Careers in Focus

SPACE EXPLORATION

Ferguson
An imprint of Infobase Publishing

Careers in Focus: Space Exploration

Ferguson
An imprint of Infobase Publishing
132 West 31st Street
New York NY 10001

ISBN-10: 0-8160-6570-5
ISBN-13: 978-0-8160-6570-7

Library of Congress Cataloging-in-Publication Data

Careers in focus. Space exploration.
    p. cm.
  Includes index.
  ISBN 978-0-8160-6570-7 (hc: alk. paper)
  1. Astronautics—Vocational guidance—Juvenile literature. I. Title: Space exploration.
  TL793.5.C37 2007
  629.4023—dc22   2006034455

Ferguson books are available at special discounts when purchased in bulk quantities for businesses, associations, institutions, or sales promotions. Please call our Special Sales Department in New York at (212) 967-8800 or (800) 322-8755.

You can find Ferguson on the World Wide Web at http://www.fergpubco.com

Text design by David Strelecky
Cover design by Joo Young An

Printed in the United States of America

MP MSRF 10 9 8 7 6 5 4 3 2 1

This book is printed on acid-free paper.

Table of Contents

Introduction

Humans have been fascinated by space ever since they first pondered the twinkling stars, watched meteorites streak through the sky, and observed other celestial phenomena. Space exploration finally became a reality in 1961, when the United States and the Soviet Union competed to put the first man in space. On April 12 of that year, Russian cosmonaut Yuri A. Gagarin became the first person to travel in space; 23 days later, American astronaut Alan Shepard became the first American to travel in space. A series of other firsts in space followed in the 1960s: John Glenn became the first American to orbit Earth in February 1962; in 1964, the Soviets placed in orbit the first spacecraft that carried more than one person; Russian cosmonaut Alexei Leonov became the first person to step outside a spacecraft in 1965; American astronauts Neil Armstrong and Edwin Aldrin Jr. became the first people to set foot on the moon.

Today, much of the work performed by the National Aeronautics and Space Administration (NASA), the U.S. agency in charge of space exploration, is directed toward improving our understanding of many biological, chemical, meteorological, and other scientific processes. Developments such as the reusable space shuttle, the Hubble Space Telescope, the International Space Station (a permanent orbiting laboratory in space), the Mars Exploration Program, and the new Crew Exploration Vehicle (which will replace the shuttle by 2011) have renewed our ambitions toward exploring space.

Countless careers are available to people interested in aerospace. Of course, when people think of space exploration, they think of a career as an astronaut. But opportunities are also available for those interested in pursuing engineering and engineering technology careers (aeronautical and aerospace technicians; aerospace engineers; avionics engineers and technicians; chemical engineers; computer engineers; industrial engineers; materials engineers; mechanical engineers; and robotics engineers and technicians), those interested in the sciences (astrobiologists, astronomers, and astrophysicists), as well as those interested in careers in clerical support, human resources, technical support, public relations, and management. There are also opportunities in education and journalism.

Earnings in space exploration range from less than $13,000 for self-employed flight instructors to more than $120,000 for experienced engineers, scientists, and pilots.

Careers in space exploration are available to those with a wide variety of educational backgrounds. For example, you will only need a high school diploma to work as an office clerk (a great way to get your foot in the door) at NASA or Boeing. Engineering technology-related careers, such as aeronautical and aerospace technician and avionics technician, typically require some postsecondary training. The majority of engineering- and science-related careers in this field require at least a bachelor's degree, with most professionals earning advanced degrees. College professors must have at least a master's degree to teach at four-year institutions, and mathematicians need a doctorate. Pilots, of course, need to complete flight training at civilian or military flight academies.

According to the U.S. Department of Labor, the aerospace product and parts manufacturing industry employed 444,000 wage and salary workers in 2004. Employment is much higher, though, as this figure does not include workers in research and development and those employed by the military and government agencies such as NASA.

Space exploration is an expensive endeavor for the U.S. government, and the program does well to maintain current funding and staffing levels. In recent years, NASA's budget has been cut more frequently than it has been maintained or increased. With continued efforts to trim the number of federal government employees, the number of government jobs in space exploration is unlikely to increase in the foreseeable future.

Many more people work for the private aerospace companies that develop and manufacture space equipment. Space exploration technology is just one sector of the aerospace industry, which covers the larger industry of commercial aircraft production. In 2005, the U.S. aerospace industry generated a record $170 billion in sales, according to the Aerospace Industries Association (AIA). The association predicts that aerospace industry sales to NASA and other nondefense federal agencies will increase during the next several years.

The AIA also predicts that aerospace companies will be looking for qualified technicians in fields such as laser optics, mission operations, spacecraft integrations, hazardous materials procedures, production planning, materials testing, computer-aided design, and robotic operations and programming. Students interested in space exploration careers may do well to take advantage of the improvement in the commercial aircraft market to gain experience that helps them gain the upper hand for the more competitive space exploration jobs in the future.

Each article in *Careers in Focus: Space Exploration* discusses a particular space exploration career in detail. The articles appear in Ferguson's *Encyclopedia of Careers and Vocational Guidance* but have been updated and revised with the latest information from the U.S. Department of Labor, professional organizations, and other sources. The articles Astrobiologists; Astrophysicists; College Professors, Aerospace/Aviation; and Writers, Aerospace/Aviation were written or extensively revised specifically for this book. The following paragraphs detail the sections and features that appear in the book.

The **Quick Facts** section provides a brief summary of the career including recommended school subjects, personal skills, work environment, minimum educational requirements, salary ranges, certification or licensing requirements, and employment outlook. This section also provides acronyms and identification numbers for the following government classification indexes: the Dictionary of Occupational Titles (DOT), the Guide to Occupational Exploration (GOE), the National Occupational Classification (NOC) Index, and the Occupational Information Network (O*NET)-Standard Occupational Classification System (SOC) index. The DOT, GOE, and O*NET-SOC indexes have been created by the U.S. government; the NOC index is Canada's career classification system. Readers can use the identification numbers listed in the Quick Facts section to access further information about a career. Print editions of the DOT (*Dictionary of Occupational Titles*. Indianapolis, Ind.: JIST Works, 1991) and GOE (*The Complete Guide for Occupational Exploration*. Indianapolis, Ind.: JIST Works, 1993) are available at libraries. Electronic versions of the NOC (http://www23.hrdc-drhc.gc.ca) and O*NET-SOC (http://online.onetcenter.org) are available on the Internet. When no DOT, GOE, NOC, or O*NET-SOC numbers are present, this means that the U.S. Department of Labor or Human Resources Development Canada have not created a numerical designation for this career. In this instance, you will see the acronym "N/A" or not available.

The **Overview** section is a brief introductory description of the duties and responsibilities involved in this career. Oftentimes, a career may have a variety of job titles. When this is the case, alternative career titles are presented. The **History** section describes the history of the particular job as it relates to the overall development of its industry or field. **The Job** describes the primary and secondary duties of the job. **Requirements** discusses high school and postsecondary education and training requirements, any certification or licensing that is necessary, and other personal requirements for success in the job. **Exploring** offers suggestions on how to gain experience in or knowledge of the particular job before making a firm educational and financial commitment. The focus is on what can be done while still in high school (or in the early years of college) to gain a better understanding of the job. The **Employers** section gives an overview of typical places of employment for the job. **Starting Out** discusses the best ways to land that first job, be it through the college placement office, newspaper ads, or personal contact. The **Advancement** section describes what kind of career path to expect from the job and how to get there. **Earnings** lists salary ranges and describes the typical fringe benefits. The **Work Environment** section describes the typical surroundings and conditions of employment— whether indoors or outdoors, noisy or quiet, social or independent. Also discussed are typical hours worked, any seasonal fluctuations, and the stresses and strains of the job. The **Outlook** section summarizes the job in terms of the general economy and industry projections. For the most part, Outlook information is obtained from the U.S. Bureau of Labor Statistics and is supplemented by information taken from professional associations. Job growth terms follow those used in the *Occupational Outlook Handbook*. Growth described as "much faster than the average" means an increase of 27 percent or more. Growth described as "faster than the average" means an increase of 18 to 26 percent. Growth described as "about as fast as the average" means an increase of 9 to 17 percent. Growth described as "more slowly than the average" means an increase of 0 to 8 percent. "Decline" means a decrease by any amount. Each article ends with **For More Information,** which lists organizations that provide information on training, education, internships, scholarships, and job placement.

Careers in Focus: Space Exploration also includes photographs, informative sidebars, and interviews with professionals in the field.

Aeronautical and Aerospace Technicians

OVERVIEW

Aeronautical and aerospace technicians design, construct, test, operate, and maintain the basic structures of aircraft and spacecraft, as well as propulsion and control systems. They work with scientists and engineers. Many aeronautical and aerospace technicians assist engineers in preparing equipment drawings, diagrams, blueprints, and scale models. They collect information, make computations, and perform laboratory tests. Their work may include working on various projects involving aerodynamics, structural design, flight-test evaluation, or propulsion problems. Other technicians estimate the cost of materials and labor required to manufacture the product, serve as manufacturers' field service technicians, and write technical materials.

HISTORY

Both aeronautical engineering and the aerospace industry had their births in the early 20th century. The very earliest machine-powered and heavier-than-air aircraft, such as the first one flown by Wilbur and Orville Wright in 1903, were crudely constructed and often the result of costly and dangerous trial-and-error experimentation.

As government and industry took an interest in the possible applications of this new invention, however, our knowledge of aircraft and the entire industry became more sophisticated. By 1908, for instance, the Wright brothers had received their first government military contract, and by 1909, the industry had expanded to include additional airplane producers, such as Glenn Curtiss in the United States and several others in France.

Aeronautical engineering and the aerospace industry have been radically transformed since those early days, mostly because of the demands of two world wars and the tremendous increases in scientific knowledge that have taken place during this century. Aviation and aerospace developments continued after the end of World War II. The factories and workers that built planes to support the war were in place and the industry took off, with the jet engine, rocket propulsion, supersonic flight, and manned voyages outside the earth's atmosphere among the major developments. As the industry evolved, aeronautical and aerospace engineers found themselves taking on increasingly larger projects and were more in need of trained and knowledgeable assistants to help them. Throughout the years, these assistants have been known as engineering aides, as engineering associates, and, most recently, as aerospace technicians and technologists. Their main task today is to take on assignments that require technical skills but do not necessarily require the scientist's or engineer's special training and education.

THE JOB

There are no clear-cut definitions of "aeronautical technology" and "aerospace technology"; in fact, many employers use the terms interchangeably. This lack of a clear distinction also occurs in education, where many schools and institutes offer similar courses under a variety of titles: aeronautical, aviation, or aerospace technology. In general, however, the term "aerospace industry" refers to manufacturers of all kinds of flying vehicles: from piston and jet-powered aircraft that fly inside the earth's atmosphere, to rockets, missiles, satellites, probes, and all kinds of manned and unmanned spacecraft that operate outside the earth's atmosphere. The term "aeronautics" is often used within the aerospace industry to refer specifically to mechanical flight inside the earth's atmosphere, especially to the design and manufacture of commercial passenger and freight aircraft, private planes, and helicopters.

The difference between technicians and technologists generally refers to their level of education. Technicians generally hold associate's degrees, while technologists hold bachelor's degrees in aeronautical technology.

Whether they work for a private company working on commercial aircraft or for the federal government, aerospace technicians work side by side with engineers and scientists in all major phases of the design, production, and operation of aircraft and spacecraft technology. The aerospace technician position includes collecting and recording data; operating test equipment such as wind tunnels and flight simulators devising tests to ensure quality control; modifying mathematical procedures to fit specific problems; laying out experimental circuits to test scientific theories; and evaluating experimental data for practical applications.

The following paragraphs describe jobs held by aerospace technicians; some of these workers may be employed in other industries as well.

Aerospace physiological technicians operate devices used to train pilots and astronauts. These devices include pressure suits, pressure chambers, and ejection seats that simulate flying conditions. These technicians also operate other kinds of flight-training equipment such as tow reels, radio equipment, and meteorological devices. They interview trainees about their medical histories, which helps detect evidence of conditions that would disqualify pilots or astronauts from further training.

Aircraft launch and recovery technicians work on aircraft carriers to operate, adjust, and repair launching and recovery equipment such as catapults, barricades, and arresting nets. They disassemble the launch and recovery equipment, replace defective parts, and keep track of all maintenance activities.

Avionics technicians repair, test, install, and maintain radar and radio equipment aboard aircraft and spacecraft.

Computer technicians assist mathematicians and subject specialists in checking and refining computations and systems, such as those required for predicting and determining orbits of spacecraft.

Drafting and design technicians convert the aeronautical engineer's specifications and rough sketches of aeronautical and aerospace equipment, such as electrical and mechanical devices, into accurate drawings that are used by skilled craft workers to make parts for aircraft and spacecraft.

Electronics technicians assist engineers in the design, development, and modification of electronic and electromechanical systems. They assist in the calibration and operation of radar and photographic equipment and also operate, install, troubleshoot, and repair electronic testing equipment.

Engineering technicians assist with review and analysis of postflight data, structural failure, and other factors that cause failure in flight vehicles.

Industrial engineering technicians assist engineers in preparing layouts of machinery and equipment, work-flow plans, time-and-motion studies, and statistical studies and analyses of production costs to produce the most efficient use of personnel, materials, and machines.

Instrumentation technicians test, install, and maintain electronic, hydraulic, pneumatic, and optical instruments. These are used in aircraft systems and components in manufacturing as well as research and development. One important responsibility is to maintain their assigned research instruments. As a part of this maintenance, they test the instruments, take readings and calibration curves, and calculate correction factors for the instruments.

Liaison technicians check on the production of aircraft and spacecraft as they are being built for conformance to specifications, keeping engineers informed as the manufacturing progresses, and they investigate any engineering production problems that arise.

Mathematical technicians assist mathematicians, engineers, and scientists by performing computations involving the use of advanced mathematics.

Mechanical technicians use metalworking machines to assist in the manufacture of one-of-a-kind parts. They also assist in rocket-fin alignment, payload mating, weight and center-of-gravity measurements, and launch-tower erection.

Target aircraft technicians repair and maintain pilotless target aircraft. They assemble, repair, or replace aircraft parts such as cowlings, wings, and propeller assemblies and test aircraft engine operation.

REQUIREMENTS

High School
A strong science and mathematics background is essential for entry into this field. High school courses that will be useful in preparing a student for college-level study include algebra, trigonometry, physics, and chemistry. In addition to math and science, courses in social studies, economics, history, blueprint reading, drafting, and industrial and machine shop practice will provide a valuable background for a career in aerospace technology. Computer experience is also important. English, speech, and courses in the preparation of test reports and technical writing are extremely helpful to develop communication ability.

Postsecondary Training
There are a variety of training possibilities for potential aerospace technicians: two-, three-, or four-year programs at colleges or universities,

junior or community colleges, technical institutes, vocational-technical schools, industry on-the-job training, or work-study programs in the military. Graduates from a two- or three-year program usually earn an associate's degree in engineering or science. Graduates from a four-year program earn a bachelor's degree in engineering or science; in addition, several colleges offer four-year degree programs in aeronautical technology. There are also many technical training schools, particularly in areas where the aerospace industry is most active, that offer training in aeronautical technology. Aircraft mechanics, for instance, usually attend one of the country's roughly 200 training schools. However, many employers require graduates of such programs to complete a period of on-the-job training before they are granted full technician status. When selecting a school to attend, check the listings of such agencies as the Accreditation Board for Engineering and Technology and the regional accrediting associations for engineering colleges. Most employers prefer graduates of an accredited school.

In general, post-high school programs strengthen the student's background in science and mathematics, including pretechnical training. Beyond that, an interdisciplinary curriculum is more helpful than one that specializes in a narrow field. Other courses that are basic to the work of the aeronautical scientist and engineer should be part of a balanced program. These include basic physics, nuclear theory, chemistry, mechanics, and computers, including data-processing equipment and procedures.

Certification or Licensing

Only a few aerospace technician positions require licensing or certification; however, certificates issued by professional organizations do enhance the status of qualified engineering technicians. Certification is usually required of those working with nuclear-powered engines or testing radioactive sources, for those working on aircraft in some test programs, and in some safety-related positions. Technicians and technologists working in areas related to national defense, and especially those employed by government agencies, are usually required to carry security clearances.

Other Requirements

Aeronautical and aerospace technicians must be able to learn basic engineering skills. They should enjoy and be proficient in mathematics and the physical sciences, able to visualize size, form, and function. The Aerospace Industries Association of America advises that today's aerospace production worker must be strong in the basics of manufacturing, have knowledge of statistics, and have the ability to work with computers.

EXPLORING

Visiting an aerospace research or manufacturing facility is one of the best ways to learn more about this field. Because there are so many such facilities connected with the aerospace industry throughout the United States, there is sure to be one in nearly every area. The reference department of a local library can help students locate the nearest facility.

Finding part-time or summer employment at such a facility is, of course, one of the best ways to gain experience or learn more about the field. Such jobs aren't available for all students interested in the field, but you can still find part-time work that will give you practical experience, such as in a local machine shop or factory.

Students should not overlook the educational benefits of visiting local museums of science and technology or aircraft museums or displays. The National Air and Space Museum at the Smithsonian Institution in Washington, D.C., is one of the most comprehensive museums dedicated to aerospace. Some Air Force bases or naval air stations also offer tours to groups of interested students. The tours may be arranged by teachers or career guidance counselors.

The Junior Engineering Technical Society (JETS) provides students a chance to explore career opportunities in engineering and technology, enter academic competitions, and design model structures. JETS administers a competition that allows students to use their technology skills. The Tests of Engineering, Aptitude, Mathematics, and Science is an open-book, open-discussion engineering problem competition. If your school doesn't have a JETS chapter, check with other schools in your area; sometimes smaller schools can form cooperatives to offer such programs.

EMPLOYERS

Aeronautical and aerospace technicians and technologists are principally employed by government agencies, commercial airlines, educational institutions, and aerospace manufacturing companies. Most technicians employed by manufacturing companies engage in research, development, and design; others work in production, sales, engineering, installation and maintenance, and other related fields. Those employed by government and educational institutions are normally assigned to do research and specific problem-solving tasks.

STARTING OUT

The best way for students to obtain an aeronautical or aerospace technician's job is through their college or university's career services office. Many manufacturers maintain recruiting relationships with schools in their area. Jobs may also be obtained through state employment offices, newspaper advertisements, applications for government employment, and industry work-study programs offered by many aircraft companies.

ADVANCEMENT

Aeronautical and aerospace technicians continue to learn on the job. As they gain experience in specialized areas, employers turn to them as experts who can solve problems, create new techniques, devise new designs, or develop practice from theory.

Most advancement involves taking on additional responsibilities. For example, with experience, a technician may take on supervisory responsibilities, overseeing several trainees, assistant technicians, or others. Such a technician may also be assigned independent responsibility, especially on some tasks usually assigned to an engineer. Technicians with a good working knowledge of the company's equipment and who have good personalities may become company sales or technical representatives. Technicians seeking further advancement are advised to continue their education. With additional formal education, a technician may become an aeronautical or aerospace engineer.

EARNINGS

Aerospace technology is a broad field, so earnings vary depending on a technician's specialty, educational preparation, and work experience. In 2005, the median annual salary for aerospace engineering and operations technicians was $52,450, according to the U.S. Department of Labor. Salaries ranged from less than $35,100 to $76,620 or more annually. Avionics technicians earned salaries that ranged from $34,620 to $60,800 or more in 2005.

Benefits depend on employers but usually include paid vacations and holidays, sick pay, health insurance, and a retirement plan. Salary increases will likely be held to a minimum over the next few years as the industry struggles to achieve a new balance after years of cutbacks and difficult markets. Nearly all companies offer some form of tuition reimbursement for further education. Some offer cooperative programs with local schools, combining classroom training with practical paid experience.

WORK ENVIRONMENT

The aerospace industry, with its strong emphasis on quality and safety, is a very safe place to work. Special procedures and equipment make otherwise hazardous jobs extremely safe. The range of work covered means that the technicians can work in small teams in specialized research laboratories or in test areas that are large and hospital-clean.

Aerospace technicians are at the launch pad, involved in fueling and checkout procedures, and back in the blockhouse sitting at an electronic console. They work in large test facilities or in specialized shops, designing and fabricating equipment. They travel to test sites or tracking stations to construct facilities or troubleshoot systems. Working conditions vary with the assignment, but the work climate is always challenging, and coworkers are well-trained, competent people.

Aeronautical technicians may perform inside activities involving confined detail work, they may work outside, or they may combine both situations. Aeronautical and aerospace technicians work in many situations: alone, in small teams, or in large groups. Commonly, technicians participate in team projects, which are coordinated efforts of scientists, engineers, and technicians working on specific assignments.

Aerospace technicians assemble the outer shell of a mockup of NASA's new Crew Exploration Vehicle. (NASA)

They concentrate on the practical aspects of the project and must get along well with and interact cooperatively with the scientists responsible for the theoretical aspects of the project.

Aerospace technicians must be able to perform under deadline pressure, meet strict requirements and rigid specifications, and deal with potentially hazardous situations. They must be willing and flexible enough to acquire new knowledge and techniques to adjust to the rapidly changing technology. In addition, technicians need persistence and tenacity, especially when engaged in experimental and research tasks. They must be responsible, reliable, and willing to accept greater responsibility.

Aerospace technology is never far from the public's attention, and aeronautical technicians have the additional satisfaction of knowing that they are viewed as being engaged in vital and fascinating work.

OUTLOOK

The *Career Guide to Industries* predicts that the aerospace products and parts manufacturing segment of the civilian aerospace industry is expected to grow by eight percent (or more slowly than the average for all occupations) through 2014 as a result of a reduction in orders for commercial transport aircraft. Employment in the military aircraft sector is expected to be better during this same time period as a result of our nation's need for more military aircraft, aerospace equipment, and related materials. Many manufacturers in the aerospace industry have responded to the decline of the 1990s by broadening their production to include other areas of technology. The Aerospace Industries Association predicts aerospace companies will be looking for qualified technicians in fields such as laser optics, mission operations, hazardous materials procedures, production planning, materials testing, computer-aided design, and robotic operations and programming.

FOR MORE INFORMATION

For a listing of accredited technology programs, visit the board's Web site or contact
   Accreditation Board for Engineering and Technology, Inc.
   111 Market Place, Suite 1050
   Baltimore, MD 21202-7116
   Tel: 410-347-7700
   http://www.abet.org

Contact the AIA for publications with information on aerospace technologies, careers, and space.
   Aerospace Industries Association (AIA)
   1000 Wilson Boulevard, Suite 1700
   Arlington, VA 22209-3928
   Tel: 703-358-1000
   http://www.aia-aerospace.org

For career information and information on student branches of this organization, contact the AIAA.
   American Institute of Aeronautics and Astronautics (AIAA)
   1801 Alexander Bell Drive, Suite 500
   Reston, VA 20191-4344
   Tel: 800-639-2422
   http://www.aiaa.org

For career and scholarship information, contact
   General Aviation Manufacturers Association
   1400 K Street, NW, Suite 801
   Washington, DC 20005-2402
   Tel: 202-393-1500
   http://www.generalaviation.org

JETS has career information and offers high school students the opportunity to "try on" engineering through a number of programs and competitions. For more information, contact
   Junior Engineering Technical Society, Inc. (JETS)
   1420 King Street, Suite 405
   Alexandria, VA 22314-2794
   Tel: 703-548-5387
   Email: info@jets.org
   http://www.jets.org

SEDS is an international organization of high school and college students dedicated to promoting interest in space. The United States national headquarters are located at the Massachusetts Institute of Technology.
   Students for the Exploration and Development of Space (SEDS)
   MIT Room W20-401
   77 Massachusetts Avenue
   Cambridge, MA 02139-4307
   Email: mitseds-officers@mit
   http://www.mit.edu/~mitseds

For more information on career choices and schools, contact
Aerospace Industries Association of Canada
60 Queen Street, Suite 1200
Ottawa, ON K1P 5Y7 Canada
Tel: 613-232-4297
Email: info@aiac.ca
http://www.aiac.ca

Aerospace Engineers

OVERVIEW

Aerospace engineering encompasses the fields of aeronautical (aircraft) and astronautical (spacecraft) engineering. *Aerospace engineers* work in teams to design, build, and test machines that fly within the Earth's atmosphere and beyond. Although aerospace science is a very specialized discipline, it is also considered one of the most diverse. This field of engineering draws from such subjects as physics, mathematics, Earth science, aerodynamics, and biology. Some aerospace engineers specialize in designing one complete machine, perhaps a commercial aircraft, whereas others focus on separate components such as for missile guidance systems. There are approximately 76,000 aerospace engineers working in the United States.

HISTORY

The roots of aerospace engineering can be traced as far back as when people first dreamed of being able to fly. Thousands of years ago, the Chinese developed kites and later experimented with gunpowder as a source of propulsion. In the 15th century, Renaissance artist Leonardo da Vinci created drawings of two devices that were designed to fly. One, the ornithopter, was supposed to fly the way birds do, by flapping its wings; the other was designed as a rotating screw, closer in form to today's helicopter.

In 1783, Joseph and Jacques Montgolfier of France designed the first hot-air balloon that could be used for manned flight. In 1799, an English baron, Sir George Cayley, designed an aircraft that was one of the first not to be considered "lighter than air," as balloons were. He developed a fixed-wing structure that led to his creation of the first glider in 1849. Much experimentation was performed in gliders and the science of aerodynamics through the late 1800s. In 1903, the first mechanically powered and controlled flight was completed in a craft designed by Orville and Wilbur Wright. The big boost in airplane development occurred during World War I. In the early years of the war, aeronautical engineering encompassed a variety of engineering skills applied toward the development of flying machines. Civil engineering principles were used in structural design, while early airplane engines were devised by automobile engineers. Aerodynamic design itself was primarily empirical, with many answers coming from liquid flow concepts established in marine engineering.

The evolution of the airplane continued during both world wars, with steady technological developments in materials science, propulsion, avionics, and stability and control. Airplanes became larger and faster. Airplanes are commonplace today, but commercial flight became a frequent mode of transportation only as recently as the 1960s and 1970s.

Robert Goddard developed and flew the first liquid-propelled rocket in 1926. The technology behind liquid propulsion continued to evolve, and the first U.S. liquid rocket engine was tested in 1938. More sophisticated rockets were eventually created to enable aircraft to be launched into space. The world's first artificial satellite, *Sputnik I*, was launched by the Soviets in 1957. In 1961, President John F. Kennedy urged the United States to be the first country to put a man on the moon; on July 20, 1969, astronauts Neil Armstrong and Edwin Aldrin Jr. accomplished that goal.

Today, aerospace engineers design spacecraft that explore beyond the Earth's atmosphere, such as space shuttles and rockets. They create missiles and military aircraft of many types, such as fighters, bombers, observers, and transports. Today's engineers go beyond the dreams of merely learning to fly. For example, in 1998, the United States and 15 other countries began a series of joint missions into space to assemble a planned International Space Station. On the ground, space professionals, including aerospace engineers, have played a vital role in developing equipment used on the station.

THE JOB

Although the creation of aircraft and spacecraft involve professionals from many branches of engineering (e.g., materials, electrical, and mechanical), aerospace engineers in particular are responsible for the total design of the craft, including its shape, performance, propulsion, and guidance control system. In the field of aerospace engineering, professional responsibilities vary widely depending on the specific job description. *Aeronautical engineers* work specifically with aircraft systems, and *astronautical engineers* specialize in spacecraft systems.

Throughout their education and training, aerospace engineers thoroughly learn the complexities involved in how materials and structures perform under tremendous stress. In general, they are called upon to apply their knowledge of the following subjects: propulsion, aerodynamics, thermodynamics, fluid mechanics, flight mechanics, and structural analysis. Less technically scientific issues must also often be dealt with, such as cost analysis, reliability studies, maintainability, operations research, marketing, and management.

There are many professional titles given to certain aerospace engineers. *Analytical engineers* use engineering and mathematical theory to solve questions that arise during the design phase. *Stress analysts* determine how the weight and loads of structures behave under a variety of conditions. This analysis is performed with computers and complex formulas.

Computational fluid dynamic (CFD) engineers use sophisticated high-speed computers to develop models used in the study of fluid dynamics. Using simulated systems, they determine how elements flow around objects; simulation saves time and money and eliminates risks involved with actual testing. As computers become more complex, so do the tasks of the CFD engineer.

Design aerospace engineers draw from the expertise of many other specialists. They devise the overall structure of components and entire crafts, meeting the specifications developed by those more specialized in aerodynamics, astrodynamics, and structural engineering. Design engineers use computer-aided design programs for many of their tasks. *Manufacturing aerospace engineers* develop the plans for producing the complex components that make up aircraft and spacecraft. They work with the designers to ensure that the plans are economically feasible and will produce efficient, effective components.

Materials aerospace engineers determine the suitability of the various materials that are used to produce aerospace vehicles. Aircraft and spacecraft require the appropriate tensile strength, density, and rigidity for the particular environments they are subjected to. Determining how materials such as steel, glass, and even chemical compounds react to temperature and stress is an important part of the materials engineer's responsibilities.

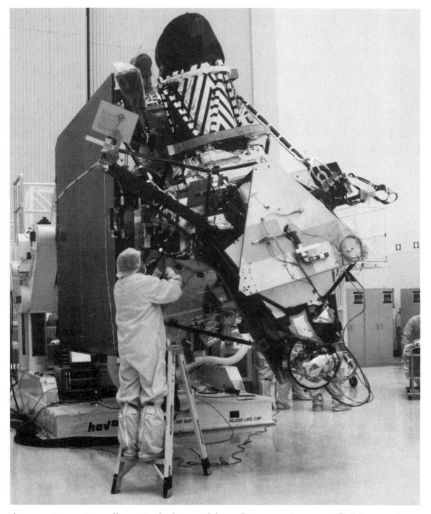

An engineer installs a gimbal on a Mars Reconnaissance Orbiter solar panel. A gimbal is an appliance that allows an object to remain horizontal even at its support tips. *(NASA)*

Quality control is a task that aerospace engineers perform throughout the development, design, and manufacturing processes. The finished product must be evaluated for its reliability, vulnerability, and how it is to be maintained and supported.

Marketing and sales aerospace engineers work with customers, usually industrial corporations and the government, informing them of product performance. They act as a liaison between the technical engineers and the clients to help ensure that the products delivered are performing as planned. Sales engineers also need to anticipate the needs of the customer, as far ahead as possible, to inform their companies of potential marketing opportunities. They also keep abreast of their competitors and need to understand how to structure contracts effectively.

REQUIREMENTS

High School
While in high school, follow a college preparatory program. Doing well in mathematics and science classes is vital if you want to pursue a career in any type of engineering field. The American Society for Engineering Education advises students to take calculus and trigonometry in high school, as well as laboratory science classes. Such courses provide the skills you'll need for problem solving, an essential skill in any type of engineering.

Postsecondary Training
Aerospace engineers need a bachelor's degree to enter the field. Advanced degrees are necessary for those interested in teaching or research and development positions.

While a major in aerospace engineering is the norm, other majors are acceptable. For example, the National Aeronautics and Space Administration recommends a degree in any of a variety of disciplines, including biomedical engineering, ceramics engineering, chemistry, industrial engineering, materials science, metallurgy, optical engineering, and oceanography. You should make sure the college you choose has an accredited engineering program. The Accreditation Board for Engineering and Technology (ABET) sets minimum education standards for programs in these fields. Graduation from an ABET-accredited school is a requirement for becoming licensed in many states, so it is important to select an accredited school. Currently, approximately 360 colleges and universities offer ABET-accredited bachelor's of engineering programs. Visit ABET's Web site (http://www.abet.org) for a listing of accredited schools.

Some aerospace engineers complete master's degrees and even doctoral work before entering this field. Advanced degrees can significantly increase an engineer's earnings. Students continuing on to graduate school will study research and development, with a thesis required for a master's degree and a dissertation for a doctorate.

Certification or Licensing

Most states require engineers to be licensed. There are two levels of licensing for engineers. Professional Engineers (PEs) have graduated from an accredited engineering curriculum, have four years of engineering experience, and have passed a written exam. Engineering graduates need not wait until they have four years experience, however, to start the licensure process. Those who pass the Fundamentals of Engineering examination after graduating are called Engineers in Training (EITs) or Engineer Interns (EIs). The EIT certification is usually valid for 10 years. After acquiring suitable work experience, EITs can take the second examination, the Principles and Practice of Engineering exam, to gain full PE licensure.

To ensure that aerospace engineers are kept up to date on their quickly changing field, many states have imposed continuing education requirements for relicensure.

Other Requirements

Aerospace engineers should enjoy completing detailed work, problem solving, and participating in group efforts. Mathematical, science, and computer skills are a must. Equally important, however, are the abilities to communicate ideas, share in teamwork, and visualize the forms and functions of structures. Curiosity, inventiveness, and a willingness to continue learning from experiences are excellent qualities to have for this type of work.

EXPLORING

If you like to work on model airplanes and rockets, you may be a good candidate for an aerospace engineering career. Consider working on special research assignments supervised by your science and math teachers for helpful experience. You may also want to try working on cars and boats, which provides a good opportunity to discover more about aerodynamics. A part-time job with a local manufacturer can give you some exposure to product engineering and development.

Exciting opportunities are often available at summer camps and academic programs throughout the country. For instance, the University of North Dakota (see address listed at the end of this article) presents an aerospace camp focusing on study and career exploration that includes instruction in model rocketry and flight. However, admission to the camp is competitive; the camp usually consists of two 10-day programs for 32 students each.

Facts About the Aerospace Industry

- Approximately 612,000 workers were employed in the aerospace products and parts industry in 2005.
- About 100,000 women were employed in the aerospace industry in 2003.
- The average hourly salary for aerospace workers was $23.89 in 2005.
- Aerospace products and parts production professionals worked an average of 42.6 hours a week in 2004—slightly higher than the average for all workers in the manufacturing industry.
- Employment in aerospace product and parts manufacturing is expected to increase by eight percent through 2014—a percentage that is slower than the average for all industries.

Sources: Aerospace Industries Association, U.S. Department of Labor

It is also a good idea to join a science club while in high school. For example, the Junior Engineering Technical Society provides members with opportunities to enter academic competitions, explore career opportunities, and design model structures. Contact information is available at the end of this article.

Aerospace America (http://www.aiaa.org/aerospace), published by the American Institute of Aeronautics and Astronautics, is a helpful magazine for exploring careers in aerospace. You should also check out the American Society for Engineering Education's pre-college Web site, http://www.engineeringk12.org/students/default.htm, for general information about careers in engineering, as well as answers to frequently asked questions about engineering. In addition, the society offers *Engineering, Go For It!*, a comprehensive brochure about careers. It is available for a small fee.

EMPLOYERS

The U.S. Department of Labor reports that approximately 76,000 aerospace engineers are employed in the United States. Many aircraft-related engineering jobs are found in Alabama, California, and Florida, where large aerospace companies are located. Nearly 60 percent of all aerospace engineers work in product and parts manufacturing. Government agencies, such as the Department of Defense and the National Aeronautics and Space Administration, employ approximately 12 percent of aerospace engineers. Other employers include engineering services, research and testing services, and electronics manufacturers.

STARTING OUT

Many students begin their careers while completing their studies through work-study arrangements that sometimes turn into full-time jobs. Most aerospace manufacturers actively recruit engineering students, conducting on-campus interviews and other activities to locate the best candidates. Students preparing to graduate can also send out resumes to companies active in the aerospace industry and arrange interviews. Many colleges and universities also staff career services centers, which are often good places to find leads for new job openings.

Students can also apply directly to agencies of the federal government concerned with aerospace development and implementation. Applications can be made through the Office of Personnel Management or through an agency's own hiring department.

Professional associations such as the National Society of Professional Engineers and the American Institute of Aeronautics and Astronautics offer job placement services, including career advice, job listings, and training. Their Web addresses are listed at the end of this article.

ADVANCEMENT

As in most engineering fields, there tends to be a hierarchy of workers in the various divisions of aerospace engineering. This is true in research, design and development, production, and teaching. In an entry-level job, one is considered simply an engineer, perhaps a junior engineer. After a certain amount of experience is gained, depending on the position, one moves on to work as a *project engineer*, supervising others. Then, as a *managing engineer*, one has further responsibilities over a number of project engineers and their teams. At the top of the hierarchy is the position of *chief engineer*, which involves authority over managing engineers and additional decision-making responsibilities.

As engineers move up the career ladder, their responsibilities generally change. Junior engineers are highly involved in technical matters and scientific problem solving. As managers and chiefs, engineers have the responsibilities of supervising, cost analyzing, and relating with clients.

All engineers must continue to learn and study technological progress throughout their careers. It is important to keep abreast of engineering advancements and trends by reading industry journals and taking courses. Such courses are offered by professional associations or colleges. In aerospace engineering especially, changes occur rapidly, and those who seek promotions must be prepared. Those employed by colleges and universities must continue teaching and conducting research if they want to have tenured (more guaranteed) faculty positions.

EARNINGS

In 2005, the median salary for all aerospace engineers was $84,090 per year, according to the U.S. Department of Labor. Experienced engineers employed by the federal government tended to earn more, with a median salary of $93,050. Federal employees also enjoy greater job security and often more generous vacation and retirement benefits. The most experienced aerospace engineers earned salaries of more than $117,680 annually.

Aerospace engineers with bachelor's degrees earned average starting salaries of $50,993 per year, according to a 2005 salary survey conducted by the National Association of Colleges and Employers. With a master's degree, candidates were offered $62,930 and with a Ph.D., $72,529.

All engineers can expect to receive vacation and sick pay, paid holidays, health insurance, life insurance, and retirement programs.

WORK ENVIRONMENT

Aerospace engineers work in various settings depending on their job description. Those involved in research and design usually work in a traditional office setting. They spend considerable time at computers and drawing boards. Engineers involved with the testing of components and structures often work outside at test sites or in laboratories where controlled testing conditions can be created.

In the manufacturing area of the aerospace industry, engineers often work on the factory floor itself, assembling components and making sure that they conform to design specifications. This job requires much walking around large production facilities, such as aircraft factories or spacecraft assembly plants.

Engineers are sometimes required to travel to other locations to consult with companies that make materials and other needed components. Others travel to remote test sites to observe and participate in flight testing.

Aerospace engineers are also employed with the Federal Aviation Administration and commercial airline companies. These engineers perform a variety of duties, including performance analyses and crash investigations. Companies involved with satellite communications need the expertise of aerospace engineers to better interpret the many aspects of the space environment and the problems involved with getting a satellite launched into space.

OUTLOOK

Employment in this field is expected to grow more slowly than the average for all occupations through 2014, according to the U.S. Department of Labor. Shrinking space program budgets, increased job efficiency, and the continuing wave of corporate downsizing have all combined to cut severely into the aerospace industry.

Nevertheless, the aerospace industry remains vital to the health of the national economy. Increasing airline traffic and the need to replace aging airplanes with quieter and more fuel-efficient aircraft will boost demand for aerospace engineers over the next decade. The federal government has increased defense budgets in order to build up the armed forces. More aerospace engineers will be needed to repair and add to the current air fleet, as well as to improve defense technology. Engineers are also needed to help make commercial aircraft safer, designing and installing reinforced cockpit doors and onboard security screening equipment to protect pilots, crew, and commercial passengers.

Despite cutbacks in the space program, the development of new space technology and increasing commercial uses for that technology will continue to require qualified engineers. Facing reduced demand in the United States, aerospace companies are increasing their sales overseas, and depending on the world economy and foreign demand, this new market could create a demand for new workers in the industry.

The U.S. Department of Labor reports that the number of students graduating with degrees in aerospace engineering has declined in recent years, and graduates will be needed to fill new positions, as well as those vacated by engineers who retire or leave the field for other careers.

FOR MORE INFORMATION

For a list of accredited schools and colleges, contact
Accreditation Board for Engineering and Technology Inc.
111 Market Place, Suite 1050
Baltimore, MD 21202-7116

Tel: 410-347-7700
http://www.abet.org

*For information about scholarships, colleges, and career opportuni-
ties, contact the following organizations:*
American Institute of Aeronautics and Astronautics
1801 Alexander Bell Drive, Suite 500
Reston, VA 20191-4344
Tel: 800-639-2422
http://www.aiaa.org

American Society for Engineering Education
1818 N Street, NW, Suite 600
Washington, DC 20036-2479
Tel: 202-331-3500
http://www.asee.org

The following organizations offer information for students.
Junior Engineering Technical Society
1420 King Street, Suite 405
Alexandria, VA 22314-2794
Tel: 703-548-5387
Email: info@jets.org
http://www.jets.org

National Society of Professional Engineers
1420 King Street
Alexandria, VA 22314-2794
Tel: 703-684-2800
http://www.nspe.org/students

For information on aerospace programs and summer camps, contact
University of North Dakota
John D. Odergard School of Aerospace Sciences
Clifford Hall, Room 512
4149 University Avenue, Stop 9008
Grand Forks, ND 58202-9008
Tel: 800-258-1525
http://www.aero.und.edu

Astrobiologists

OVERVIEW

Astrobiologists, also known as *exo-biologists, life scientists,* and *space scientists,* study the origin of all life forms—from a simple one-celled organism, to plants, to human beings. They study and research the evolution, distribution, and future of these life forms, on Earth as well as on other planets in our solar system and beyond. Many astrobiologists are employed by the National Aeronautics and Space Administration (NASA) and other government-funded agencies. They are also employed at private research institutions and colleges and universities.

HISTORY

Throughout the course of history, humans have been interested in science. Taxonomy, the science of classifying living things, was practiced whenever farmers chose to plant certain seeds they found superior to others. Ecology, the study of living things in relation to their environment, was practiced as farmers learned to rotate their crops, in order to better take care of the soil and produce strong crop yields. Simple principles of genetics, the science of genes and heredity, was applied by Gregor Mendel during his crossbreeding experiments. Many more scientists and inventors through the centuries have used the principles of chemistry, physics, biology, and mathematics to help understand the history of people, animals, and plants, as well as help improve the quality of everyday life.

Astrobiology, the study of the origin, development, and distribution of all forms of life, grew from many different specialties of life

QUICK FACTS

School Subjects
Biology
Physiology

Personal Skills
Mechanical/manipulative
Technical/scientific

Work Environment
Indoors and outdoors
Primarily multiple locations

Minimum Education Level
Bachelor's degree

Salary Range
$33,151 to $60,190 to $99,020+

Certification or Licensing
None available

Outlook
About as fast as the average

DOT
041

GOE
02.02.03

NOC
2121

O*NET-SOC
19-1021.00, 19-1022.00, 19-1023.00, 19-1029.00

and Earth science. Its name is derived from the Greek words *astron* (star), *bios* (life), and *logos* (science). As astrobiologists seek to find how life began and how it is affected by evolution and environment, they use the ideas, techniques, and philosophy of such sciences as geology, astronomy, chemistry, microbiology, molecular biology, biogeochemistry, and oceanography. They use the same concepts to study whether life exists on other planets. In fact, most astrobiologists receive their early education and training in other sciences before specializing in the field of astrobiology.

Only a few universities in the United States offer graduate programs in astrobiology. One of these, the University of Washington, offers the only doctoral program geared to find and study life in outer space. Private research institutes, such as the SETI Institute, employ astrobiologists to staff research projects such as understanding the biosphere of Mars or how perennial hot springs exist in the Canadian Arctic. Many astrobiologists work at NASA's research institutes, including the Ames Research Institute in California.

In 1995, NASA organized the NASA Astrobiology Institute (NAI) a partnership between the government agency, academic institutes, and research centers throughout the United States. Today, about 700 scientists, researchers, and educators work together at the NAI to learn more about the living universe.

THE JOB

Astrobiologists study the origin, evolution, distribution, and future of all life forms in the universe. Astrobiologists' work is varied—they try to find answers to such questions as how life forms are affected by changes in environment, if any forms of life exist on other planets, as well as the adaptability of human beings to extraterrestrial environments.

Most work for government-funded agencies such as NASA. For example, at NASA's Ames Research Center, astrobiologists could be assigned to work on research projects covering animal muscle evolution or plant adaptation. Much of their work takes place inside a laboratory with actual specimens, but sometimes the nature of their research takes them to different places around the world. Some are even assigned to help plan and monitor experiments for future spaceflight missions.

Many other astrobiologists find work at the university level, either as researchers or educators. Academic positions are quite competitive, since only a few schools offer programs devoted to astrobiology. However, this may change in the near future as interest grows in this interdisciplinary field.

Astrobiologists also work at private research institutes located worldwide. An astrobiologist employed as a researcher at the Scripps Institute, for example, might conduct studies on the effects of drastic environments on simple proteins. Researchers strive to have their work published in industry journals such as *Astrobiology Magazine* or presented at seminars offered by the NAI.

REQUIREMENTS
High School
Are you signed up for freshman year Earth science? This and related courses will provide you with a solid foundation for your future career. Other classes to consider are biology, chemistry, physics, geology, botany, and mathematics. Also consider nonscience courses such as speech and English, or any classes that can sharpen your communication skills. What's the point of knowing everything there is to know about algae or hydrothermal springs if you can't convey your ideas to others?

Postsecondary Training
Astrobiology is an interdisciplinary science, and as such, scientists, researchers, and educators working in this field come from a variety of educational backgrounds, with undergraduate degrees ranging from biology to chemistry to astronomy. Some astrobiologists, especially those doing laboratory work, may find employment with a bachelor's degree. However, the majority of top researchers, and certainly those teaching at universities, have earned or are in the process of completing their Ph.D's. A small number of universities—such as the University of California-Los Angeles (http://www.ess.ucla.edu/research/astrobio.asp), the University of Washington (http://dcpts.washington.edu/astrobio), Arizona State University (http://astrobiology.asu.edu), and the University of Colorado (http://lasp.colorado.edu/life) offer graduate programs or coursework in astrobiology. Also, annual conferences for astrobiology graduate students, such as the one held by Arizona State University, can provide information on new programs starting at other universities.

Other Requirements
Astrobiologists must be systematic in their approach to solving problems. They should have probing, inquisitive minds and an aptitude for biology, geology, chemistry, astronomy, microbiology, molecular biology, biogeochemistry, oceanography, and mathematics. Patience and imagination are also required, since they may spend much time

in observation and analysis. Astrobiologists must also have good communication skills in order to gather and exchange data and solve problems that arise in their work.

EXPLORING

Students can measure their aptitude and interest in the work of the astrobiologist by taking biology courses. Laboratory assignments, for example, provide information on techniques used by the working astrobiologist. Many schools hire students as laboratory assistants to work directly under a teacher and help administer the laboratory sections of courses.

School assemblies, field trips to federal and private laboratories and research centers, and career conferences provide additional insight into career opportunities. Advanced students often are able to attend professional meetings and seminars.

Part-time and summer positions in biology or related areas are particularly helpful. Students with some college courses in biology and astrobiology may find summer positions as laboratory assistants. Graduate students may find work on research projects conducted by their institutions. Beginning college and advanced high school students may find employment as laboratory aides or hospital orderlies or attendants. Despite the menial nature of these positions, they afford a useful insight into careers in biology and astrobiology. High school students often have the opportunity to join volunteer service groups at local hospitals. Student science training programs at colleges and universities allow qualified high school students to spend a summer doing research under the supervision of a scientist.

EMPLOYERS

Slightly more than half of all biological scientists work for the government at the federal, state, or local level. Astrobiologists are employed by the National Aeronautics and Space Administration and other government-funded agencies. They also work at private research institutions and colleges and universities.

STARTING OUT

Students interested in becoming teachers should consult their college career services offices. An increasing number of colleges hire teachers through the colleges at which they studied. Some teaching positions are filled through direct application.

Astrobiologists interested in private industry and nonprofit organizations may also apply directly for employment. Major organizations such as NASA that employ astrobiologists often interview
college seniors on campus. Private and public employment offices
frequently have listings from these employers. Experienced astrobiologists may change positions as a result of contacts made at professional seminars and national conventions.

Special application procedures are required for positions with
government agencies. Civil service applications for federal, state,
and municipal positions may be obtained by writing to the agency
involved and from high school and college guidance and placement
bureaus, public employment agencies, and post offices.

ADVANCEMENT

To a great extent, advancement for astrobiologists depends on the
individual's level of education. A doctorate is generally required for
college teaching, independent research, and top-level administrative
and management jobs. A master's degree is sufficient for some jobs
in applied research, and a bachelor's degree may qualify for some
entry-level jobs.

With the right qualifications, the astrobiologist may advance to the
position of project chief and direct a team of other astrobiologists.
Many use their knowledge and experience as background for administrative and management positions. Often, as they develop professional
expertise, astrobiologists move from strictly technical assignments
into positions in which they interpret astrobiological knowledge.

EARNINGS

Earnings for astrobiologists vary extensively based on the type and
size of their employer and the individual's level of education and
experience. The U.S. Department of Labor does not provide salary
information for astrobiologists, but it does report that the median
salary for all biological scientists was $60,190 in 2005. Salaries
ranged from less than $33,430 to more than $99,020. In 2005, general biological scientists working for the federal government earned
a mean salary of $66,550. Scientists employed by NASA earned
starting salaries that ranged from $33,151 to $44,034 in 2006.

Astrobiologists are usually eligible for health and dental insurance, paid vacations and sick days, and retirement plans. Some
employers may offer reimbursement for continuing education, seminars, and travel.

WORK ENVIRONMENT

The astrobiologist's work environment varies greatly, depending upon the position and type of employer. One astrobiologist may work outdoors or travel much of the time. Another may wear a white smock and spend years working in a laboratory. Some work with toxic substances and disease cultures; strict safety measures must be observed.

OUTLOOK

The U.S. Department of Labor predicts that employment for all biological scientists will grow as fast as the average through 2014, although competition will be stiff for some positions. For example, Ph.D.s looking for research positions will find strong competition for a limited number of openings. In addition, certain government jobs as well as government funding for research may also be less plentiful. A recession or shift in political power can cause the loss of funding for grants and the decline of research and development endeavors.

Astrobiologists with advanced degrees will be best qualified for the most lucrative and challenging jobs. Scientists with bachelor's degrees may find openings as science or engineering technicians or as health technologists and technicians.

FOR MORE INFORMATION

For information on careers in biology, contact
American Institute of Biological Sciences
1444 I Street, NW, Suite 200
Washington, DC 20005-6535
Tel: 202-628-1500
Email: admin@aibs.org
http://www.aibs.org

For a career brochure, career-related articles, and a list of institutions that award academic degrees with a major in physiology, contact
American Physiological Society
9650 Rockville Pike
Bethesda, MD 20814-3991
Tel: 301-634-7164
http://www.the-aps.org

For information on careers, educational resources, and fellowships, contact
American Society for Microbiology
1752 N Street, NW
Washington, DC 20036-2904
Tel: 202-737-3600
http://www.asm.org

The NASA Astrobiology Institute is focused on the xenobiologic study of the living universe. For information on its current research projects, fellowships, and other educational opportunities, contact
NASA Astrobiology Institute
Tel: 650-604-0809
http://nai.arc.nasa.gov

The Scripps Research Institute is the largest private, nonprofit research organization in the United States. Its research is biomedically focused. To learn more about the institute's research projects currently in progress at its California or Florida facilities, or to obtain information regarding the doctorate program, contact
Scripps Research Institute
10550 North Torrey Pines Road
La Jolla, CA 92037-1000
Tel: 858-784-1000
http://www.scripps.edu

This magazine features monthly "hot topics" ranging from extrasolar life to terrestrial origins. Its online version also offers a forum, a collection of astrobiology images, and news of the latest advancements in the field of astrobiology.
Astrobiology
http://www.astrobio.net

Visit the following Web site to learn more about exobiology:
Exobiology: Life Through Space and Time
http://exobiology.arc.nasa.gov

INTERVIEW

Dr. Jack Farmer directs the Astrobiology Program at Arizona State University in Tempe, Arizona. He discussed his career and the education of astrobiology students with the editors of Careers in Focus: Space Exploration.

Q. What is astrobiology?

A. Astrobiology is a developing area of science that has been defined as the field that studies the origin, evolution, distribution, and future of life in the Solar System. This is an interdisciplinary effort that involves many different types of scientists (e.g. planetary geologists, astronomers, biologists, biogeochemists, cosmochemists, etc.) all working collaboratively.

Q. Tell us about your career as an astrobiologist.

A. I was trained as a paleobiologist/sedimentary geologist and early on became interested in the ways that organisms interact with sediments to create biologically influenced sedimentary rocks. Sedimentary rocks are those that form by the weathering and transport of other rocks and are our main source of information about ancient environments on Earth, while preserving a fossil record of terrestrial life. I have always been fascinated by the early history of life on Earth, and this was my route to study it. Since I first began these studies as a graduate student, the field has grown and developed many new methods of inquiry. For example, in recent years, paleobiologists have expanded their studies to include the microbial world. Microbes dominated the first 85 percent of Earth's history, up until the first complex multicelled life (plants and animals) appeared in the fossil record. Collectively, microbes still run the planet, mediating most major biogeochemical cycles. This idea was captured in the concept of Gaia: the Earth as a living organism that buffers extreme changes in climate and other environmental changes through biological processes. While I don't advocate the extreme views of Gaia (I see this phenomenon as integrative ecology on a planetary scale), the concept is useful in pointing out how the life that we rarely see controls many of the most important aspects of planetary evolution. I have carried many of my interests about how life has developed and evolved on Earth to the field of planetary science by asking how our understanding of life here (the one place in the cosmos to date, where we know life developed) can inform our exploration for life on other planets and moons in our Solar System and beyond. This "Earth as analog" approach to exploration for life elsewhere is a central aspect of astrobiology.

Q. What is one of your most interesting achievements as an astrobiologist?

A. Our studies of the geomicrobiology of extreme environments (hydrothermal springs and salty, alkaline lakes) have been especially enlightening in opening new vistas and approaches to the exploration for life elsewhere in the Solar System and on the early Earth. My ongoing interest in exploring for Martian life has fueled my long-term involvement in Mars mission planning, which I think has helped the National Aeronautics and Space Administration (NASA) make better decisions about how to approach the astrobiological exploration of the Red Planet. Being a member of the Mars Exploration Rover team has certainly been a highlight of my career to date, and I am looking forward to also participating in the Mars Science Laboratory mission that will be launched in 2009.

Q. Tell us about the astrobiology program at Arizona State University (ASU).
A. Arizona State University maintains a highly interdisciplinary program in astrobiology that involves faculty and students from fields as diverse as geological sciences, astronomy, microbiology, molecular biology, biogeochemistry, and oceanography. The program mainly consists of a dynamic portfolio of NASA-sponsored research in the above fields and an evolving curriculum that presently consists of introductory and graduate-level courses in astrobiology and cross-bridging fields, like biogeochemistry and geomicrobiology. The program, which is an integral part of the new School of Earth and Space Exploration at ASU, has benefited a great deal from direct association of many of its supporting faculty with NASA missions to Mars, the outer Solar System, and beyond (through the Hubble Space Telescope). Currently, astrobiology students at ASU receive their degrees in one or more of the above fields. While we presently offer no formal degrees in astrobiology, we expect to establish a minor degree program in astrobiology in the 2007-08 timeframe and eventually an interdisciplinary studies degree leading to graduate (M.S. and Ph.D.) degrees in astrobiology.

Q. What are the most important personal and professional qualities for astrobiology students?
A. Students who do well in astrobiology are those who possess an innate curiosity about life and its origins. They are attracted to the interfaces between fields and to the excitement and new discoveries that come from transdisciplinary studies in science.

They train broadly in science and are not afraid to cross discipline boundaries in their work.

Q. Where do astrobiology graduates find work?

A. At present in the U.S., students who train in astrobiology receive their degrees in one of the traditional, established fields of science (e.g., chemistry, geology, astronomy, etc.) and then apply their interests through teaching and research in one of the main theme areas of astrobiology (e.g., origin of life studies, early Earth and Solar System studies, planetary exploration, astronomy, cosmochemistry, etc.). Most of these students find employment at academic institutions around the world (as teachers and researchers in the above fields), as contract researchers working for government-sponsored labs, or by working for NASA (e.g., planetary mission specialists, astronomers, and researchers).

Q. What is the future employment outlook for astrobiologists?

A. It seems clear that human interest in the question of life elsewhere and in the basic exploration of space is not just a passing fancy. In fact, the U.S. (through NASA, military, and commercial ventures), as well as the other spacefaring nations of the world, will in all likelihood continue to expand their quest to explore the Solar System and beyond, with an increasing need for students trained in astrobiology. This growth may be gradual, depending on national priorities, but growth is, I believe, inevitable. So, while the job market may remain competitive, it will continue and, with time, will expand.

Astronauts

OVERVIEW

Astronauts conduct experiments and gather information while in space flight. They also conduct experiments with the spacecraft itself to develop new concepts in design, engineering, and the navigation of a vehicle outside the Earth's atmosphere.

HISTORY

When the U.S. space program began in 1959, there were only seven astronauts in the entire country. There are 95 astronauts and 11 candidates currently in the U.S. space program. In total, 321 astronauts have been selected in the 19 groups from 1959 through 2004.

The first person to travel in space was a Russian, Yuri A. Gagarin, on April 12, 1961. The United States quickly followed suit, launching Alan Shepard, the first U.S. astronaut, into space on May 5, 1961. These men may have been the first to experience space, but the work of other pioneers made space travel possible. Robert H. Goddard of the United States and Hermann Oberth of Germany are recognized as the fathers of space flight. It was Goddard who designed and built a number of rocket motors and ground-tested the liquid fuel rocket. Oberth published *The Rocket into Interplanetary Space* in 1923, which discussed technical problems of space and described what a spaceship would be like. Although there were few significant advances beyond this until after World War II, the Soviets and Germans did carry on experiments in the 1930s, and it was quite evident in the 1940s that space flights were to become a reality.

The U.S. space program began operations on October 1, 1958, when the National Aeronautics and Space Administration (NASA) was created. NASA was created largely in response to Soviet success at launching the world's first artificial satellite in 1957. The United States and Soviet Union continued space flights through the 1960s. Astronauts practiced maneuvering spacecraft and working in space on these missions. There were several firsts in this decade also: The Soviet Union placed the first spacecraft with more than one person into space in 1964; in 1965, Russian cosmonaut Alexei Leonov became the first person to step outside a spacecraft. NASA's first goal, to put a man on the moon by the end of the 1960s, was accomplished in 1969 when Neil Armstrong and Edwin Aldrin, Jr., were the first people to set foot on the moon. Both countries continued developing their programs throughout the 1970s, when astronauts carried out the first repair work in space.

During the 1970s, it became evident that a space station—a permanent orbiting laboratory in space in which astronauts could come and go and work from—could be a reality. The concept of a staffed outpost in Earth orbit has been something people have imagined for years. In May 1973, the United States launched the *Skylab* space station. *Skylab* hosted crews for stays of 28, 56, and 84 days and proved that humans could live and work in space for extended periods. Crews conducted medical tests and made astronomical, solar, and Earth observations. However, *Skylab* was not designed for resupply or refueling and was brought back to Earth in 1979.

In the 1980s, the United States began working with 15 other countries to plan what became the International Space Station. The United States launched the first reusable manned spacecraft, the space shuttle *Columbia*. The Soviets also began using space shuttles during the 1980s and launched their version of a space station, *Mir*. Despite the progress of recent decades, however, both countries were still learning. On January 28, 1986, the U.S. space shuttle *Challenger* exploded shortly after takeoff, killing all seven crew members. (Tragedy struck the space shuttle program again on February 1, 2003, when the *Columbia* broke up during reentry into the Earth's atmosphere, killing all seven crewmembers.)

In late 1998, the Russian aerospace program delivered the first component of the International Space Station (ISS). An initial crew of three began living aboard the space station in late 2000. Construction on the ISS is expected to continue for at least the next several years.

In 2005, NASA announced that it planned to retire the space shuttle and create a new spacecraft via its Constellation Program. The new spacecraft, the Crew Exploration Vehicle, is expected to be ready by 2011. It will be used to ferry astronauts and cargo to the ISS and explore the Moon, Mars, and beyond. (Visit http://www. nasa.gov/mission_pages/exploration/spacecraft/index.html for more information on the Constellation Program.)

THE JOB

The major role of astronauts is carrying out research; they conduct engineering, medical, and scientific experiments in space. Astronauts also operate and maintain the spacecraft that carries them and launch and recapture satellites. In the early days of space flight, spacecraft could contain only one or two astronauts. Today, a team of astronauts, each with specific duties for the flight, works aboard space shuttles and space stations.

Astronauts are part of a complex system. Throughout the flight, they remain in nearly constant contact with Mission Control and various tracking stations around the globe. Space technology experts on the ground monitor each flight closely, even checking the crew members' health via electrodes fitted to their bodies. *Flight directors* provide important information to the astronauts and help them solve any problems that arise.

The basic crew of a space shuttle is made up of at least five people: the *commander*, the *pilot*, and three *mission specialists*, all of whom are NASA astronauts. Some flights also call for a payload specialist, who becomes the sixth member of the crew. From time to time, other experts will be on board. Depending on the purpose of the mission, they may be engineers, technicians, physicians, or scientists such as astronomers, meteorologists, or biologists. Now that the International Space Station (ISS) has become operable, crews may vary more, as astronauts who specialize in different areas come and go from the space station on space shuttles. Up to seven astronauts at a time are able to live and work on the space station.

The commander and the pilot of a space shuttle are both pilot astronauts who know how to fly aircraft and spacecraft. Commanders are in charge of the overall mission. They maneuver the orbiter and supervise the crew and the operation of the vehicle. In addition, they are responsible for the success and safety of the flight. Pilots help the commanders control and operate the orbiter and may help manipulate satellites by using a remote control system. Like other crew members, they sometimes do work outside the craft or look after the payload.

Mission specialists are also trained astronauts. They work along with the commander and the pilot. Mission specialists work on specific experiments, perform tasks outside the orbiter, use remote manipulator systems to deploy payloads, and handle the many details necessary to carry out the mission. One or more *payload specialists* may be included on flights. A payload specialist may not be a NASA astronaut but is an expert on the cargo being carried into space.

Although much of their work is conducted in space, astronauts are involved in extensive groundwork before and during launchings. Just prior to lift-off, they go through checklists to be sure nothing has been forgotten. Computers on board the space shuttle perform the countdown automatically and send the vehicle into space. When the rocket boosters are used up and the external fuel tank becomes empty, they separate from the orbiter. Once in orbit, the astronauts take control of the craft and are able to change its position or course or to maneuver into position with other vehicles.

The research role of astronauts has expanded with the operation of the ISS. The station provides the only laboratory free of gravity where scientific research can be conducted. Such an environment unmasks the basic properties of materials, and astronauts conduct experiments that may lead to new manufacturing processes on Earth. Scientists have high expectations for medical research that astronauts have conducted aboard the space station. It is hoped that such research will help fight diseases such as influenza, diabetes, and AIDS. In conducting such tests, astronauts operate a number of special cameras, sensors, meters, and other highly technical equipment.

Another important part of an astronaut's work is the deployment of satellites. Communications satellites transmit telephone calls, television programs, educational and medical information, and emergency instructions. Other satellites are used to observe and predict weather, to chart ocean currents and tides, to measure the earth's various surfaces and check its natural resources, and for defense-related purposes. Satellites released from a shuttle can be propelled into much higher orbits than the spacecraft itself is capable of reaching, thus permitting a much wider range of observation. While on their missions, astronauts may deploy and retrieve satellites or service them. Between flights, as part of their general duties, astronauts may travel to companies that manufacture and test spacecraft components, where they talk about the spacecraft and its mission.

Astronaut training includes instruction in all aspects of space flight and consists of classroom instruction in astronomy, astrophysics, meteorology, star navigation, communications, computer theory, rocket engines and fuels, orbital mechanics, heat transfer, and space medicine. Laboratory work will include training in space-flight simulators, during which many of the actual characteristics of space flight are simulated along with some of the emergencies that may occur in flight. To ensure their safety while in flight, astronauts also learn to adjust to changes in air pressure and extreme heat and observe their physical and psychological reactions to these changes. They need to be prepared to respond to a variety of possible circumstances.

REQUIREMENTS

High School

High school students interested in a career as an astronaut should follow a regular college preparatory curriculum in high school but should endeavor to do as much work as possible in mathematics and science. Preparing to get into a good college is important, because NASA takes into consideration the caliber of a college program when accepting astronaut candidates. Earning high scores on standardized tests (ACT or SAT) will also help you get into a good college program.

Postsecondary Training

Any adult man or woman in excellent physical condition who meets the basic qualifications can be selected to enter astronaut training, according to NASA. The basic requirements are U.S. citizenship and a minimum of a bachelor's degree in engineering, biological or physical science, or mathematics. There is no age limit, but all candidates must pass the NASA space-flight physical. Beyond these basic requirements, there may be additional requirements, depending on the astronaut's role. NASA specifies further requirements for two other types of astronauts: the mission specialist and the pilot astronaut.

Mission specialists are required to have at least a bachelor's degree in one of four areas of specialty (engineering, biological science, physical science, or mathematics), although graduate degrees are preferred. In addition, candidates must have at least three years of related work experience. Advanced degrees can take the place of part or all of the work experience requirements. Mission specialists must pass a NASA space physical, which includes the following standards: 20/200 or better distance visual acuity, correctable to 20/20 in each eye, blood pressure no higher than 140/90, and height between 58.5 and 76 inches.

There are three major requirements for selection as a pilot astronaut candidate. A bachelor's degree in one of the four areas of specialty is required; an advanced degree is desirable. Candidates must also be jet pilots with at least 1,000 hours of pilot-in-command time in jet aircraft. Pilot astronauts must also pass a physical, with

20/100 or better distance visual acuity, correctable to 20/20 in each eye, blood pressure no higher than 140/90, and height between 64 and 76 inches. Because of the flight-time requirement, it is rare for a pilot astronaut to come from outside the military.

Astronaut candidates undergo a year-long testing period. During this time, they are examined for how well they perform under zero-gravity conditions, in laboratory conditions, and as a member of a team with other candidates. If candidates are able to pass this first year, they are given astronaut status, and their training as astronauts begins.

Other Requirements

Astronauts must be highly trained, skilled professionals with a tremendous desire to learn about outer space and to participate in the highly dangerous exploration of it. They must have a deep curiosity with extremely fine and quick reactions. They may have to react in emergency conditions that may never before have been experienced; to do so, they must be able to remain calm and to think quickly and logically. As individuals, they must be able to respond intelligently to strange and different conditions and circumstances.

EXPLORING

Students who wish to become astronauts may find it helpful to contact various organizations concerned with space flights. There are lots of books available on space exploration, both in your school and city library.

The Internet also has several excellent sites on space exploration. NASA's Web site (http://nasajobs.nasa.gov/astronauts) is user friendly, with biographies of actual astronauts, advice on becoming an astronaut, and news about current NASA projects. Other interesting sites include Ask the Space Scientist, in which astronomer Dr. Sten Odenwald answers questions at http://image.gsfc.nasa.gov/poetry/ask/askmag.html, and space image libraries such as those found at NASA's National Space Science Data Center (http://nssdc.gsfc.nasa.gov/photo_gallery).

The National Air and Space Museum (http://www.nasm.si.edu) at the Smithsonian Institution in Washington, D.C., is an excellent way to learn about space exploration history. There are also several NASA-run space, research, and flight centers all over the country. Most have visitor centers and offer tours.

There are also space camps for high school students and older people all over the nation. These camps are not owned or operated by NASA, so the quality of their programs can vary greatly. Your high school counselor can help you find more information on space camps in your area.

EMPLOYERS

All active astronauts are employed by NASA, although some payload specialists may also be employed elsewhere, such as at a university or private company. All are NASA-trained and paid. Within the NASA program, astronauts may be classified as civil service employees or military personnel, depending on their background. Astronauts who gain astronaut status through their military branch remain members of that military branch and maintain their rank. Astronauts who go to college and test into the program are civil service employees.

Inactive or retired astronauts may find employment opportunities outside NASA. Jobs might include teaching at a university, conducting research for other government agencies or private companies, working with manufacturers to develop space equipment, and educating the public on the space program.

STARTING OUT

You can begin laying the groundwork toward making your astronaut application stand out from others when you are in college. Those who have been successful in becoming astronauts have distinguished themselves from the hundreds of other applicants by gaining practical experience. Internships and work/study positions in your chosen area of interest are a good way to gain vital experience. Your college placement office can help direct you to such opportunities. Working on campus as a teacher assistant or research assistant in a lab is another good way to make yourself more marketable later on.

Once other qualifications are met, a student applies to become an astronaut by requesting and filling out U.S. Government Application Form 171 from NASA, Johnson Space Center, Attn: Astronaut Selection Office, Mail Code AHX, 2101 NASA Parkway, Houston, TX 77058-3696. The form is reviewed at the Johnson Space Center, where all astronauts train. The application will be ranked according to height considerations, experience, and expertise. Active duty military applicants do not apply to NASA. Instead, they submit applications to their respective military branch. Entrance into the profession is competitive. Aspiring astronauts compete with an average of 4,000 applicants for an average of 20 slots that open up every two years, according to NASA. From the pool of 4,000 applicants, roughly 118 are asked to come to the Johnson Space Center for a week of interviews, medical examinations, and orientation.

From there, the Astronaut Selection Board interviews applicants and assigns them a rating. Those ratings are passed on to a NASA administrator, who makes the final decision.

Entrance into the profession involves extensive piloting or scientific experience. Those hoping to qualify as pilot astronauts are encouraged to gain experience in all kinds of flying; they should consider military service and attempt to gain experience as a test pilot. People interested in becoming mission specialist astronauts should earn at least one advanced degree and gain experience in one or more of the accepted fields (engineering, biological or physical science, and mathematics).

ADVANCEMENT

Advancement is not a formal procedure. Astronauts who are members of the military generally rise in rank when they become astronauts and as they gain experience. Those employed by the civil service may rise from the GS-11 to GS-13 rating. Those who gain experience as astronauts will likely work into positions of management as they retire from actual flight status. Some astronauts may direct future space programs or head space laboratories or factories. Some astronauts return to military service and may continue to rise in rank. As recognized public figures, astronauts can enter elected office and enjoy government and public speaking careers.

EARNINGS

For most, the attraction to being an astronaut is not the salary—and with good reason. The field is one of the most rewarding, but astronauts don't draw large salaries. Astronauts begin their salaries in accordance with the U.S. Government pay scale. Astronauts enter the field at a minimum classification of GS-11, which in 2006 paid a minimum of $46,189, according to the Office of Personnel Management General Schedule. As they gain experience, astronauts may advance up the classification chart to peak at GS-13, which pays between $65,832 and $85,578. Of course, there are opportunities outside NASA (although these don't involve space flight) that may pay higher salaries. Astronauts who go to work in the private sector can often find positions with universities or private space laboratories that pay six-figure salaries.

In addition, astronauts get the usual benefits, including vacations, sick leave, health insurance, retirement pensions, and bonuses for superior performance. Salaries for astronauts who are members of the armed forces consist of base pay, an allowance for housing and subsistence, and flight pay.

An astronaut performs maintenance during a space walk. *(NASA)*

WORK ENVIRONMENT

Astronauts do work that is difficult, challenging, and potentially dangerous. They work closely as a team because their safety depends on their being able to rely on one another. They work a normal 40-hour week when preparing and testing for a space flight. As countdown approaches and activity is stepped up, however, they may work long hours, seven days a week. While on a mission, of course, they work as many hours as necessary to accomplish their objectives.

The training period is rigorous, and conditions in the simulators and trainers can be restrictive and uncomfortable. Exercises to produce the effect of weightlessness may cause air sickness in new trainees.

Astronauts on a space flight have to become accustomed to floating around in cramped quarters. Because of the absence of gravity, they must eat and drink either through a straw or very carefully with fork and spoon. Bathing is accomplished with a washcloth, as there are no showers in the spacecraft. Astronauts buckle and zip themselves into sleep bunks to keep from drifting around the cabin. Sleeping is generally done in shifts, which means that lights, noises, and activity are a constant factor.

During the launch and when working outside the spacecraft, astronauts wear specially designed spacesuits to protect them against various facets of the new environment.

OUTLOOK

Only a very small number of people will ever be astronauts. NASA chooses its astronauts from an increasingly diverse pool of applicants. From thousands of applications all over the country, approximately 100 men and women are chosen for an intensive astronaut training program every two years. The small number of astronauts is not likely to change in the near future. Space exploration is an expensive venture for the governments that fund it, and often the program does well to maintain current funding levels. Great increases in funding, which would allow for more astronauts, are highly unlikely. While the ISS project has generated increased public interest and will likely continue to do so as discoveries are reported, the project still requires only a small number of astronauts at a time aboard the station.

Much of the demand will depend on the continued success of the space station and other programs and how quickly they develop. The satellite communications business is expected to grow as private industry becomes more involved in producing satellites for commercial use. But these projects are not likely to change significantly the employment picture for astronauts in the immediate future.

FOR MORE INFORMATION

For information on space launches, the International Space Station, and other educational resources, contact
Kennedy Space Center
Public Inquiries
Kennedy Space Center, FL 32899
Tel: 321-449-4444
http://www.ksc.nasa.gov

For information on aeronautical careers, internships, and student projects, contact the information center or visit NASA's Web site.
National Aeronautics and Space Administration (NASA)
Public Communications and Inquiries Management Office,
  Suite 1M32
Washington, DC 20546-0001
Tel: 202-358-0001
Email: public-inquiries@hq.nasa.gov
http://www.nasa.gov

Astronomers

OVERVIEW

Astronomers study the universe and its celestial bodies by collecting and analyzing data. They also compute positions of stars and planets and calculate orbits of comets, asteroids, and artificial satellites. Astronomers make statistical studies of stars and galaxies and prepare mathematical tables giving positions of the Sun, Moon, planets, and stars at a given time. They study the size and shape of the Earth and the properties of its upper atmosphere through observation and through data collected by spacecraft and Earth satellites. There are approximately 800 astronomers employed in the United States.

HISTORY

The term *astronomy* is derived from two Greek words: *astron*, meaning star, and *nemein*, meaning to arrange or distribute. It is one of the oldest sciences. The field has historically attracted people who have a natural fascination with our universe. Astronomers have traditionally been driven by a desire to learn; for many, the pursuit of practical applications of astronomy has been secondary.

One of the earliest practical applications, the establishment of a calendar based on celestial movement, was pursued by many ancient civilizations, including the Babylonians, Chinese, Mayans, Europeans, and Egyptians. A chief aim of early astronomers was to study the motion of the bodies in the sky in order to create a calendar that could be used to predict certain celestial events and provide a more orderly structure to social life. The ancient Babylonians were among the first to construct a calendar based on the movement of the sun and the phases of the moon; their calendar has been found to have been accurate within minutes. In Europe, stone mounds constructed by ancient inhabitants also attest to astronomical work. Stonehenge is one of the largest and most famous of these mounds.

Ancient Greek astronomers introduced a new concept of astronomy by attempting to identify the physical structure of the universe, a branch of astronomy that has become known as *cosmology*. Astronomers such as Aristotle, Apollonius, Hipparchus, and Ptolemy succeeded in describing the universe in terms of circular movements. Their discoveries and theories were adopted by astronomers throughout much of the world. Modern astronomy was born with the theory of the sun-centered universe, first proposed by Nicolaus Copernicus in the 16th century. Copernicus's discovery revolutionized the field of astronomy and later would have a dramatic impact on many aspects of science.

After thousands of years, astronomers had succeeded in developing accurate predictions of celestial events. Next, they turned to newly evolving areas of astronomy, those of identifying the structure of the universe and of understanding the physical nature of the bodies they observed. Astronomers were aided by the invention of telescopes, and, as these increased in power, astronomers began to make new discoveries in the skies. For much of history, for example, it was believed that there were only five planets in the solar system. By the end of the 17th century, that number had increased to six; over the next two centuries, three more planets (Neptune, Uranus, and Pluto) were discovered. In 2006 the International Astronomical Union's new definition of what constitutes a planet stripped Pluto of planet status, reclassifying it as a dwarf planet.

Astronomers have always relied heavily on tools to bring faraway worlds close enough for study. As technology has evolved, so then has the field of astronomy. Spectroscopy, invented in the 19th century, allowed astronomers to identify the elements that make up the composition of the planets and other celestial bodies and gave rise to a new branch of astronomy, called *astrophysics*, which describes the components of the universe by measuring such information as temperature, chemical composition, pressure, and density. Later, photography, too, became an important research aid. In the early years of the 20th century, new discoveries further revolutionized the field of astronomy, particularly with the discovery of other galaxies beyond our own. The understanding grew that the universe was constructed of many millions of galaxies, each an island in an infiniteness of space.

By the middle of the 20th century, scientists had learned how to send rockets, and later manned spacecraft, into space to gain a closer view of the universe surrounding us. Using satellites and unmanned space probes, astronomers have been able to travel far into the solar system, toward the most distant planets. A major event in astronomy occurred with the launching in 1990 of the powerful Hubble Space Telescope, which orbits the Earth and continues to send back information and photographs of events and phenomena across the universe.

THE JOB

Astronomers study the universe and all of its celestial bodies. They collect and analyze information about the moon, planets, sun, and stars, which they use to predict their shapes, sizes, brightness, and motions.

They are interested in the orbits of comets, asteroids, and even artificial satellites. Information on the size and shape, the luminosity and position, the composition, characteristics, and structure as well as temperature, distance, motion, and orbit of all celestial bodies is of great relevance to their work.

Practical application of activity in space is used for a variety of purposes. The launching of space vehicles and satellites has increased the importance of the information astronomers gather. For example, the public couldn't enjoy the benefits of accurate weather prediction if satellites weren't keeping an eye on our atmosphere. Without astronomical data, satellite placement wouldn't be possible. Knowledge of the orbits of planets and their moons, as well as asteroid activity, is also vital to astronauts exploring space.

Astronomers are usually expected to specialize in some particular branch of astronomy. The *astrophysicist* is concerned with applying the concepts of physics to stellar atmospheres and interiors. (For more information, see the article "Astrophysicists.") *Radio astronomers* study the source and nature of celestial radio waves with extremely sensitive radio telescopes. The majority of astronomers either teach or do research or a combination of both. Astronomers in many universities are expected to teach such subjects as physics and mathematics in addition to astronomy. Other astronomers are engaged in such activities as the development of astronomical instruments, administration, technical writing, and consulting.

Astronomers who make observations may spend long periods of time in observatories. Astronomers who teach or work in laboratories may work eight-hour days. However, those who

An astronomer points to the polar hood of Mars in a picture he took.
(Reuters/Landov)

make observations, especially during celestial events or other peak viewing times, may spend long evening hours in observatories. Paperwork is a necessary part of the job. For teachers, it can include lesson planning and paper grading. Astronomers conducting research independently or for a university can expect to spend a considerable amount of time writing grant proposals to secure funding for their work. For any scientist, sharing the knowledge acquired is a vital part of the work. Astronomers are expected to painstakingly document their observations and eventually combine them into a coherent report, often for peer review or publication.

Although the telescope is the major instrument used in observation, many other devices are also used by astronomers in carrying out these studies, including spectrometers for the measurement of wavelengths of radiant energy, photometers for the measurement of light intensity, balloons for carrying various measuring devices, and computers for processing and analyzing all the information gathered.

Astronomers use ground-based telescopes for night observation of the skies. The Hubble Space Telescope (http://hubblesite.org), which magnifies the stars at a much greater percentage than land-based capability allows, has become an important tool for the work of many astronomers.

REQUIREMENTS
High School
While in high school, prospective astronomers should take mathematics (including analytical geometry and trigonometry), science courses (including chemistry and physics), English, foreign languages, and courses in the humanities and social sciences. Students should also be well grounded in the use of computers and in computer programming.

Postsecondary Training
All astronomers are required to have some postsecondary training, with a doctoral degree being the usual educational requirement because most jobs are in research and development. A master's degree is sufficient for some jobs in applied research and development, and a bachelor's degree is adequate for some nonresearch jobs. Students should select a college program with wide offerings in physics, mathematics, and astronomy and take as many of these courses as possible. Graduate training will normally take at least three years beyond the bachelor's degree.

Bachelor's degrees in astronomy are offered by about 80 institutions in the United States, and 40 institutions offer master's degrees or doctorates in the field, often combined with physics departments. Some of the astronomy courses typically offered in graduate school are celestial mechanics, galactic structure, radio astronomy, stellar atmospheres and interiors, theoretical astrophysics, and binary and variable stars. Some graduate schools require that an applicant for a doctorate spend several months in residence at an observatory. In most institutions the student's graduate courses will reflect his or her chosen astronomical specialty or particular field of interest.

Other Requirements
The field of astronomy calls for people with a strong but controlled imagination. They must be able to see relationships between what may appear to be, on the surface, unrelated facts, and they must be able to form various hypotheses regarding these relationships. Astronomers must be able to concentrate over long periods of time. They should also express themselves well verbally and in writing.

EXPLORING

A number of summer or part-time jobs are usually available in observatories. The latter may be either on a summer or year-round

Learn More About It

Barnes-Svarney, Patricia L., and Michael R. Porcellino. *Through the Telescope: A Guide for the Amateur Astronomer.* 2nd ed. New York: McGraw-Hill, 1999.

Bortz, Fred. *Beyond Jupiter: The Story of Planetary Astronomer Heidi Hammel.* Washington, D.C.: J. Henry Press, 2006.

Chartrand, Mark. *The Night Sky: A Guide to Field Identification.* New York: St. Martin's Press, 2001.

Harrington, Philip S. *Star Ware: The Amateur Astronomer's Ultimate Guide to Choosing, Buying, & Using Telescopes and Accessories.* 3rd ed. San Francisco: Jossey-Bass, 2002.

VanCleave, Janice. *Janice VanCleave's Solar System: Mind-Boggling Experiments You Can Turn Into Science Fair Projects.* San Francisco: Jossey-Bass, 2000.

basis. These jobs not only offer experience in astronomy but often act as stepping stones to good jobs upon graduation. Students employed in observatories might work as guides or as assistants to astronomers.

Students can test their interest in this field by working part time, either as an employee or as a volunteer, in planetariums or science museums. Many people enjoy astronomy as a hobby, and there are a number of amateur astronomy clubs and groups active throughout the country. Amateur astronomers have often made important contributions to the field of astronomy. In 1996, for example, a new comet was discovered by an amateur astronomer in Japan. Students may gain experience in studying the skies by purchasing, or even building, their own telescopes.

Reading or using the Internet to learn more on your own is also a good idea. What about astronomy interests you? You can find specific information in books or on the Internet. Check out NASA's Web site at http://www.nasa.gov. It contains useful information about careers in astronomy and aeronautics and information about current space exploration. Another interesting Web site is http://www.absoluteastronomy.com, which contains information on planets, constellations, nebulas, galaxies, and other topics. When you hear in the news that a comet or meteor shower will be visible from Earth, be sure to set your alarm to get up and watch and learn. Science teachers will often discuss such events in class.

EMPLOYERS

Approximately one-third of all physicists and astronomers work for scientific research and development companies. Another 25 percent work for the federal government. Astronomers represent only a small portion of these workers. The federal government employs astronomers in agencies such as NASA, the U.S Naval Observatory, the U.S. Department of Defense, and the Naval Research Laboratory.

Astronomers more frequently find jobs as faculty members at colleges and universities or are affiliated with those institutions through observatories and laboratories. Other astronomers work in planetariums, in science museums, or in other public service positions involved in presenting astronomy to the general public; others teach physics or Earth sciences in secondary schools or are science journalists and writers.

In the private sector, astronomers are hired by consulting firms that supply astronomical talent to the government for specific tasks. In addition, a number of companies in the aerospace industry hire astronomers to work in related areas in order to use their background and talents in instrumentation, remote sensing, spectral observations, and computer applications.

STARTING OUT

A chief method of entry for astronomers with a doctorate is to register with the college's placement bureau, which provides contacts with one of the agencies looking for astronomers. Astronomers can also apply directly to universities, colleges, planetariums, government agencies, aerospace industry manufacturers, and others who hire astronomers. Many positions are advertised in professional and scientific journals devoted to astronomy and astrophysics.

Graduates with bachelor's or master's degrees can normally obtain semiprofessional positions in observatories, planetariums, or some of the larger colleges and universities offering training in astronomy. Their work assignments might be as research assistants, optical workers, observers, or technical assistants. Those employed by colleges or universities might well begin as instructors. Federal government positions in astronomy are usually earned on the basis of competitive examinations. Jobs with some municipal organizations employing astronomers are often based on competitive examinations. The examinations are usually open to those with bachelor's degrees.

NASA offers internships for students with some postsecondary training. To find out more about NASA internships and other opportunities, explore its Web site: http://www.nasajobs.nasa.gov.

ADVANCEMENT

Because of the relatively small size of the field, advancement may be somewhat limited. A professional position in a large university or governmental agency is often considered the most desirable post available to an astronomer because of the opportunities it offers for additional study and research. Those employed in colleges may well advance from instructor to assistant professor to associate professor and then to professor. There is also the possibility of eventually becoming a department head.

Opportunities also exist for advancement in observatories or industries employing people in astronomy. In these situations, as in those in colleges and universities, advancement depends to a great extent on the astronomer's ability, education, and experience. Peer recognition, in particular for discoveries that broaden the understanding of the field, is often a determinant of advancement. Publishing articles in professional journals, such as *Scientific American* or the *Journal of Astrophysics and Astronomy,* is a way for astronomers to become known and respected in the field. Advancement isn't usually speedy; an astronomer may spend years devoted to a specific research problem before being able to publish conclusions or discoveries in a scientific journal.

EARNINGS

According to the U.S. Department of Labor, astronomers had median annual earnings of $104,670 in 2005. Salaries ranged from less than $49,920 to $142,220 or more annually. The average for astronomers employed by the federal government in 2005 was $115,290, according to the U.S. Department of Labor.

In educational institutions, salaries are normally regulated by the salary schedule prevailing in that particular institution. As the astronomer advances to higher-level teaching positions, his or her salary increases significantly.

Opportunities also exist in private industry for well-trained and experienced astronomers, who often find their services in demand as consultants. Fees for this type of work may run as high as $200 per day in some of the more specialized fields of astronomy.

WORK ENVIRONMENT

Astronomers' activities may center on the optical telescope. Most telescopes are located high on a hill or mountain and normally in a fairly remote area, where the air is clean and the view is not affected by lights from unrelated sources. There are approximately 300 of these observatories in the United States.

Astronomers working in these observatories usually are assigned to observation from three to six nights per month and spend the remainder of their time in an office or laboratory, where they study and analyze their data. They also must prepare reports. They may work with others on one segment of their research or writing and then work entirely alone on the next. Their work is normally carried on in clean, quiet, well-ventilated, and well-lighted facilities.

Those astronomers in administrative positions, such as director of an observatory or planetarium, will maintain fairly steady office hours but may also work during the evening and night. They usually are more involved in administrative details, however, spending less time in observation and research.

Those employed as teachers will usually have good facilities available to them, and their hours will vary according to class hours assigned. Work for those employed by colleges and universities may often be more than 40 hours per week.

OUTLOOK

The U.S. Department of Labor predicts that employment for astronomers will grow more slowly than the average for all occupations through 2014. Astronomy is one of the smallest science fields. Job openings result from the normal turnover when workers retire or leave the field for other reasons. Competition for these jobs, particularly among new people entering the profession, will continue to be strong. In recent years, the number of new openings in this field has not kept pace with the number of astronomers graduating from the universities, and this trend is likely to continue for the near future. Furthermore, there will likely be few new positions made, since funding in this area is hard to come by.

The federal government will continue to provide employment opportunities for astronomers. Defense expenditures are expected to increase over the next decade, and this should provide stronger employment opportunities for astronomers who work on defense-related research projects. However, government agencies, particularly NASA, may find their budgets reduced in the coming years, and the number of new positions created for astronomers will likely drop as well. Few new observatories will be constructed, and those currently in existence are not expected to greatly increase the size of their staffs.

The greatest growth in employment of astronomers is expected to occur in business and industry. Companies in the aerospace field will need more astronomers to do research to help them develop new equipment and technology.

FOR MORE INFORMATION

Visit the FAQ section of this association's Web site to read the online article Career Profile: Astronomy.
American Association of Amateur Astronomers
PO Box 7981
Dallas, TX 75209-0981
Email: aaaa@astromax.com
http://www.corvus.com

To read A New Universe to Explore: A Guide to Careers in Astronomy, *visit the AAS's Web site.*
American Astronomical Society (ASA)
2000 Florida Avenue, NW, Suite 400
Washington, DC 20009-1231
Tel: 202-328-2010
Email: aas@aas.org
http://www.aas.org

For a list of print and online resources about astronomy, contact
Astronomical Society of the Pacific
390 Ashton Avenue
San Francisco, CA 94112-1722
Tel: 415-337-1100
http://www.astrosociety.org

This organization is a resource for professionals who work in many physics disciplines, including astronomy. For more information, contact
American Institute of Physics
1 Physics Ellipse
College Park, MD 20740-3843
Tel: 301-209-3100
Email: aipinfo@aip.org
http://www.aip.org

━━━━━━ INTERVIEW ━━━━━━

Dr. Heidi Hammel is a planetary astronomer and the co-director of the Research Branch at the Space Science Institute in Boulder, Colorado. She discussed her career with the editors of Careers in Focus: Space Exploration.

Q. What made you want to become a space scientist?

A. It was the most fun of all the things I tried in college. I went to Massachusetts Institute of Technology (MIT) as an undergraduate with absolutely no intention of doing astronomy. I just happened to take a course in astronomy as a sophomore and liked it.

But there are two things that I remember from when I was a kid that probably contributed to my later interest in astronomy. One is that I used to get car sick, and my parents used to take us on trips a lot in the car and so I had to lie on the back seat being sick, and the only thing I could do was look out the window and see the stars. And so I learned the constellations, I learned what the bright stars were, and that's what kept me going on those long car trips. And the second thing I remember, when I was a kid, is going to a planetarium. They would do a star show about what the stars looked like and what constellations were visible that night. That was all kind of boring, but at some point during the show a "comet" would streak across the sky with flames and a roar that was really loud, and you never knew when it was going to happen, and that was really exciting. And I would go back to the planetarium again and again and again just to wait for that comet to come. I think I probably picked up a little astronomy along the way when I was doing that. (I have learned since then that comets are actually giant balls of ice that usually move very slowly and very silently across the sky.)

Q. Tell us about your work at the Space Science Institute? What are your research interests?

A. I am an astronomer, more specifically a planetary astronomer or planetary scientist. My business card says "Senior Research Scientist." I primarily study outer planets and their satellites, with a focus on observational techniques. I am an expert about the planet Neptune, and was a member of the Imaging Science Team for the Voyager 2 encounter with that planet in 1989. For the impact of Comet Shoemaker-Levy 9 with Jupiter in July 1994, I led the Hubble Space Telescope (HST) Team that investigated Jupiter's atmospheric response to the collisions. My latest research involves studies of Neptune and Uranus with HST and other Earth-based observatories. I am an interdisciplinary scientist for HST's successor, the James Webb Space Telescope, which is scheduled for launch in 2013. I am also serving on the Science and Technology Definition Team for NASA's Terrestrial Planet Finder Coronograph mission, which may launch in 2015.

Since my job is so multi-faceted, I find it difficult to describe a typical day. But certainly, a typical day does not include observing with a telescope. That is a misconception, and not how most astronomers' hours are spent. Most of the time, I work at a computer analyzing data, computing models, or writing papers. I also travel a lot to attend meetings or to make observations. Reviewing other scientists' proposals (for NASA and National Science Foundation programs) and articles (submitted for publication in professional journals) are also part of the daily routine. I spend lots of time writing grant proposals.

Most astronomers hold teaching positions at colleges and universities, combining teaching and research. Teaching and preparing for class consume a great deal of time for this type of astronomer and finding time for research is sometimes difficult. Other astronomers work at research institutions. This kind of astronomer can spend up to half of their time carrying out their own programs of research, and the remainder doing things such as developing new instrumentation or supporting archives of data from instruments.

Yet other astronomers carve out their own career paths, and this is becoming more common as the traditional careers have been less available. I work for a nonprofit organization that has the dual mission of excellence in scientific research and excellence in education and public outreach. So my time is balanced between my research and doing things like this—answering questions from the public about astronomy!

Q. What type of educational path did you pursue to become a space scientist?

A. When I was involved in the 1994 Comet Crash into Jupiter, the TV station near where I went to high school sent a crew down to Baltimore to interview me. They asked me what was the most important course I took in high school. I answered, "Chorus." It taught me to approach everything from a professional point of view—"No amateur-land in Dixie," my choral teacher would always proclaim. That attitude is critical for success.

I also took as much as my high school had to offer: physics, calculus, and chemistry. I avoided biology, though, since I didn't want to be involved in dissecting things. Just a personal choice.

You should take a typing course because astronomers do a lot of work with computers and writing. Also take English and make certain you can write clearly, formulate essays, spell, and logically present an issue based on well-reasoned arguments and evidence. Scientists are a dime a dozen today; scientists who can actually communicate effectively are much rarer. And to be completely frank, the sciences in general are a tough field to survive in in today's budget-cutting world, so having excellent communication skills on top of good scientific qualifications is a real plus.

Personally, I wasn't involved in any science clubs or things like that. I did music—band, chorus, orchestra, musical theatre. I won the band award my senior year (I played pitched percussion instruments, tympani, chimes, bells, xylophone, etc.) My advice is: Do what you like and do it well!

I went to college (MIT) as an undergraduate with absolutely no intention of doing astronomy. I just happened to take a course in astronomy as a sophomore and liked it. The rest is history.

Q. What are the most important personal and professional qualities for space scientists?

A. Just as each person is different, each space science career is different. There are no "required" personal skills. Physically there is really not much of a limitation—look at Stephen Hawking; so much is done with computers now, not only theory but even observation, that physical limitations are becoming less and less a problem. With respect to knowledge, Einsteins are one in a million. The rest of us just work very, very hard. That's the most important thing: Be prepared to work hard!

Q. What advice would you offer students as they graduate and look for jobs in this field?

A. In the field of "traditional" astronomy, most people expect to end up working as professors at colleges or universities. Since the number of astronomers has gone up while the number of faculty positions has gone down, it's not a sure bet that a young person will find a stable job. Most of us are spending years in multiple post-doctoral positions or end up working in "soft-money" non-tenure-track jobs (this is the type of job I have right now; it means my job is never secure, and I have to spend most of my time writing proposals to NASA or the National Science Foundation to bring in enough funding to pay my salary). Nevertheless, there are still a few jobs here and they are scattered around the world, and with hard work and luck and a willingness to travel, a motivated young person can succeed in that traditional path. Because the "traditional" path is becoming less practical, many young astronomers are looking into alternative careers. Since astronomers are strongly skilled in computing, programming, and Internet skills, they have market potential in e-business, in the financial world, as programmers, and in other types of computer-related jobs. For an idea of the current job market, students should take a quick glance at the American Astronomical Society's Job Register for this month's listings (http://members. aas.org/JobReg/Jobregister.cfm). This will provide an idea of the types of jobs available, the salaries, and the locations.

Q. What is the future employment outlook in aerospace and related fields?

A. I don't have a crystal ball, and my Magic 8 Ball variously says "Reply hazy, try again," or "Outlook not so good," or even "Better not tell you now" (the scariest reply). I can say that the nature of jobs in astronomy is changing as more temporary positions lasting one to two years, at low salary, are offsetting the traditional secure positions (tenured professorships or government civil service jobs). Most of us are constantly under stress to find funding. Many young astronomers may get a "post-doc" after a long hard battle to get a Ph.D. and then find their careers terminated because there were no openings for them. Even us "middle-agers" have these stresses, because after 10 or 15 years as active researchers, some of us may find ourselves too expensive for what we do than younger astronomers willing to do nearly the same work at 20 to 30 percent lower salaries and with less experience. The other stress is the repeated forecasts that the NASA space research budget will be declining by over 30 percent in the next seven years. For many astronomers, NASA grants are the lifeblood of an astronomy career! That said, NASA and space science are part of the American landscape, so astronomy and aeronautics will continue at some level. The key to a successful career is the ability to work hard, make good choices, and be an excellent communicator.

Astrophysicists

OVERVIEW

Astrophysics is a specialty that combines two fields of science: astronomy and physics. *Astrophysicists* use the principles of physics to study the solar system, stars, galaxies, and the universe. How did the universe begin? How is the universe changing? These are the types of questions astrophysicists try to answer through research and experimentation. Physicists may also be concerned with such issues, but they use physics to study broader areas such as gravity, electromagnetism, and nuclear interactions.

HISTORY

Astrophysics began in the 1800s, when astronomers developed the spectroscope, which is used to determine the various properties of stars and planets. In spectroscopy, light is spread into a spectrum, and the resulting image can be used to determine a star's chemical composition, temperature, surface condition, and other properties. Astrophysicists knew that understanding the nature of stars would help them understand the larger question that all astrophysicists work toward answering: How did the universe begin?

A major advance in the field of astrophysics was the development of atomic theory. In 1803, a British chemist, John Dalton, proposed that each natural element consists of a particular kind of atom. In the early 1900s, scientists discovered that each atom has a nucleus, which contains protons, neutrons, and electrons that interact with each other. Today, the atom is the basis of the study of physics. Physicists of all disciplines, from astrophysicists to nuclear physicists, use what we know about the atom and its parts to understand their respective fields.

Hubble Space Telescope

The Hubble Space Telescope, which was named after American astronomer Edwin P. Hubble, is the world's first space-based optical telescope. It was launched into space in 1990 by the Space Shuttle *Discovery*. Hubble has allowed us to gather a wealth of new information about planets, our solar system, our galaxy, and countless other space objects and phenomena. Here are some interesting facts about the Hubble Space Telescope:

- Length: 43.5 feet, or as long as a large school bus

- Weight: 24,500 pounds, or as heavy as two adult elephants

- Cost at launch: $1.5 billion

- Distance above the Earth: 370 miles

- Speed: 17,500 mph. It takes 97 minutes to orbit the Earth.

  Nothing lasts forever, and this adage is also true with Hubble. Sometime after 2010, Hubble will cease to function. Space scientists are currently working on a replacement for Hubble: the James Webb Space Telescope. This new telescope will have 10 times the power of the Hubble Space Telescope. Visit http://www.jwst.nasa.gov for more information on this new telescope.

Source: Hubblesite

In the case of astrophysicists, close examination of the parts of the atom will help to understand how matter and our universe formed. A widely held explanation today is the "Big Bang" theory, which hypothesizes that the universe was formed 15 to 20 billion years ago when a dense singular point of matter exploded and eventually formed stars and galaxies. Today, most astrophysicists believe the universe is still expanding from that initial explosion.

THE JOB

To do their work, astrophysicists need access to large, expensive equipment, such as radio telescopes, spectrometers, and specialized computers. Because this equipment is generally available only at universities with large astronomy departments and government observatories, most astrophysicists are employed by colleges or the government.

A primary duty of most astrophysicists is making and recording observations. What they observe and the questions they are trying to answer may vary, but the process is much the same across the profession. They work in observatories, using telescopes and other equipment to view celestial bodies. They record their observations on charts or, more often today, into computer programs that help them analyze the data.

Astrophysicists work to understand the beginning and end of the lives of stars. They use spectrometers, telescopes, and other instruments to measure infrared radiation, ultraviolet radiation, and radio waves. They study not only the formation of stars but also whether planets formed along with them. Understanding the lives of stars will help astrophysicists understand the origins and future of the universe. Their work is often tedious, requiring multiple measurements over time. The answer to one question, such as the age of a specific star, often leads to more questions about nearby planets and other formations. To address these larger questions, astrophysicists from all over the world must work together to come to agreements.

Most astrophysicists who work for universities also teach. Depending on their branch of research, teaching may be their primary duty. Astrophysicists share their findings with the scientific community. They often travel to conferences to speak about their findings and to listen to other scientists discuss techniques or research. Discoveries are also shared in professional journals, such as *The Astrophysical Journal*. Many scientists spend time compiling their data and writing articles for such journals.

REQUIREMENTS

High School

If you are interested in becoming an astrophysicist, concentrate on classes in mathematics and science. If they are available, take classes at an advanced level to better prepare for challenging college courses. English skills are also important because astrophysicists must write up their results, communicate with other scientists, and lecture on their findings. Finally, make sure you are comfortable working with computers either by taking a computer science class or by exploring on your own.

Postsecondary Training

An advanced degree is highly desirable for a career in astrophysics. A few who have bachelor's degrees in physics, astronomy, or mathematics may work as research assistants in the field. To do your own research or teach, you should have at least a master's degree, with a Ph.D. preferred for full astrophysicists.

Other Requirements

Because astrophysicists deal with abstract concepts and faraway celestial bodies, an active imagination and the ability to draw logical conclusions from observational data are helpful traits. Some research can be tedious and take long periods of time; astrophysicists must be patient in their work and have the ability to remain focused and meet deadlines.

Astrophysicists who have a natural curiosity about why things occur no doubt enjoy their work most when research or experiments culminate in a discovery that will help them and others in the field gain a larger understanding of the universe.

EMPLOYERS

Because astrophysicists require such expensive equipment to do their job, their employers are generally limited to large colleges or government agencies. Some government agencies that employ astrophysicists include the National Aeronautics and Space Administration (NASA), the U.S. Naval Observatory, and Fermi National Accelerator Laboratory, a physics laboratory known as Fermilab. Fermilab is the home of the world's most powerful particle accelerator, which scientists from various institutions use to conduct research to better understand energy and the atom.

According to the U.S. Department of Labor, there are approximately 16,000 physicists and astronomers working in the United States. Most work for scientific research and development services firms. Approximately 25 percent work for the federal government, mostly with the Department of Defense and NASA. Others work for colleges or universities, either as faculty members or in nonfaculty research positions. These scientists work all over the country, but most are employed in areas where large universities or research laboratories are located.

STARTING OUT

Many astrophysicists get their first paying job as graduate students who assist professors in astronomy, physics, or astrophysics. These assistant jobs are known in the field as postdoctoral positions. Students may help the professors grade undergraduate and graduate papers or assist them in recording and compiling astronomical data in the observatory.

Beginning jobs in government may include internships or temporary positions with specific research projects. The job market for astrophysicists is very competitive; students and recent graduates often must volunteer their time at university or government observatories and work other jobs until they can find full-time, paid work.

ADVANCEMENT

Astrophysicists work with other highly educated people, including mathematicians, astronomers, and other scientists. Astrophysicists who work for large universities or the government should have a sense of the "department politics," and be able to deal diplomatically with department heads and colleagues competing for resources such as grants and equipment.

At the beginning of their careers, astrophysicists may be assigned to work nights at the observatory. Hours can be long, and pay can be limited. After they have gained experience, astrophysicists can expect to be involved in the planning and development stages of research and may not be required to do as much observation and data recording. With further experience, astrophysicists can advance to become tenured professors, research institution leaders, or observatory managers.

EARNINGS

Salaries for astrophysicists tend to parallel those listed for astronomers and physicists because of their job similarities. According to the U.S. Department of Labor, the median annual salary of physicists was $89,810 in 2005. The lowest-paid 10 percent earned less than $49,070, and the highest-paid 10 percent earned over $136,870.

The American Institute of Physics reported the following median earnings for physicists by degree level in 2004: Ph.D.s (excluding those in postdoctoral positions), $104,000; master's degrees, $94,000; and bachelor's degrees, $72,000.

WORK ENVIRONMENT

Astrophysicists generally work regular hours in laboratories, observatories, or classrooms. However, some research may require them to work extended or irregular hours. A research deadline or a celestial event such as a meteor shower or asteroid may require extra hours or overnight observation. Some travel may be required and is generally paid for by the astrophysicist's employer, such as to an observatory with a needed piece of equipment or to a conference or training.

Astrophysicists work with other highly educated professionals, such as mathematicians, astronomers, and other scientists. The work environment can be competitive and sometimes political because these professionals often compete for the same limited resources.

OUTLOOK

The outlook for astrophysics, because it is so closely related to astronomy and physics, mirrors the outlook for those fields. According to the U.S. Department of Labor, employment in these fields will grow slower than the average for all occupations through 2014. The need for scientists, especially those employed by the government, is affected by factors outside the field, such as budgetary cuts and political issues that draw attention (and funding) away from expensive research programs.

Aspiring astrophysicists should be prepared for a tight job market, especially in research positions. Within private industry, many companies are reducing their amount of basic research (which includes physics-related research) in favor of applied research and software development. Job openings for engineers and computer scientists will far outnumber those for physicists and astrophysicists.

FOR MORE INFORMATION

This is an organization for professionals who work in different areas of physics, including astrophysicists. For more information, contact
American Institute of Physics
1 Physics Ellipse
College Park, MD 20740-3843
Tel: 301-209-3100
Email: aipinfo@aip.org
http://www.aip.org

For additional information on the field of astronomy, contact
American Astronomical Society
2000 Florida Avenue, NW, Suite 400
Washington, DC 20009-1231
Tel: 202-328-2010
Email: aas@aas.org
http://www.aas.org

To read articles on astrophysics, check out the following Web site:
The Astrophysical Journal
http://www.journals.uchicago.edu/ApJ

Avionics Engineers and Technicians

OVERVIEW

Avionics (from the words *aviation* and *electronics*) is the application of electronics to the operation of aircraft, spacecraft, and missiles. *Avionics engineers* conduct research and solve developmental problems associated with aviation, such as instrument landing systems and other safety instruments. Avionics engineering is a sub-specialty of the field of aerospace engineering. There are approximately 76,000 aerospace engineers in the United States.

Avionics technicians inspect, test, adjust, and repair the electronic components of aircraft communications, navigation, and flight-control systems and compile complete maintenance-and-overhaul records for the work they do. Avionics technicians also calibrate and adjust the frequencies of communications apparatus when it is installed and perform periodic checks on those frequency settings. Approximately 22,500 avionics technicians are employed in the United States.

HISTORY

The field of avionics grew out of World War II, when military aircraft were operated for the first time using electronic equipment. Rockets were also being developed during this time, and these devices required electronic systems to control their flight. As aircraft rapidly grew more complicated, the amount of electronic apparatus needed for navigation and for monitoring equipment performance greatly increased. The World

War II B-29 bomber carried 2,000 to 3,000 avionic components; the B-52 of the Vietnam era carried 50,000; later, the B-58 supersonic bomber required more than 95,000. As the military grew increasingly reliant on electronic systems, specialists were required to build, install, operate, and repair them.

The development of large ballistic missiles during and after World War II and the rapid growth of the U.S. space program after 1958 increased development of avionics technology. Large missiles and spacecraft require many more electronic components than even the largest and most sophisticated aircraft. Computerized guidance systems became especially important with the advent of manned spaceflights. Avionics technology was also applied to civil aircraft. The race to be the first in space, and later, to be the first to land on the moon, stimulated the need for more and more trained specialists to work with newer and more complex electronic technology. The push for achieving military superiority during the Cold War era also created a demand for avionics specialists and technicians. From the 1950s to the present, the commercial airline industry grew rapidly; more and more planes were being built, and the drive to provide greater comfort and safety for passengers created still greater demand for avionics engineers and technicians.

Avionics continues to be an important branch of aeronautical and astronautical engineering. The aerospace industry places great emphasis on research and development, assigning a much higher percentage of its trained technical personnel to this effort than is usual in industry. In addition, stringent safety regulations require constant surveillance of in-service equipment. For these reasons there is a high demand for trained and experienced avionics engineers and technicians to help in the development of new satellites, spacecraft, aircraft, and their component electronic systems and to maintain those in service.

THE JOB

Avionics engineers develop new electronic systems and components for aerospace use. Avionics technicians assist engineers in these developments. They also adapt existing systems and components for application in new equipment. For the most part, however, they install, test, repair, and maintain navigation, communications, and control apparatus in existing aircraft and spacecraft.

Technicians use apparatus such as circuit analyzers and oscilloscopes to test and replace such sophisticated equipment as transceivers and Doppler radar systems, as well as microphones, headsets, and other standard electronic communications apparatus. New equipment, once installed, must be tested and calibrated to prescribed specifications. Technicians also adjust the frequencies of radio sets and other communications equipment by signaling ground stations and then adjusting set screws until the desired frequency has been achieved. Periodic maintenance checks and readjustments enable avionics technicians to keep equipment operating on proper frequencies. The technicians also complete and sign maintenance-and-overhaul documents recording the history of various equipment.

Avionics engineers and technicians involved in the design and testing of a new apparatus must take into account all operating conditions, determining weight limitations, resistance to physical shock, the atmospheric conditions the device will have to withstand, and other factors. For some sophisticated projects, technicians will have to design and make their tools first and then use them to construct and test new avionic components.

The range of equipment in the avionics field is so broad that technicians usually specialize in one area, such as radio equipment, radar, computerized guidance, or flight-control systems. New specialty areas are constantly opening up as innovations occur in avionics. The development of these new specialty areas requires technicians to keep informed by reading technical articles and books and by attending seminars and courses about the new developments, which are often sponsored by manufacturers.

Avionics technicians usually work as part of a team, especially if involved in research, testing, and development of new products. They are often required to keep notes and records of their work and to write detailed reports.

REQUIREMENTS

High School
Persons interested in pursuing a career in avionics should take high school mathematics courses at least through solid geometry and preferably through calculus. They should take English, speech, and communications classes in order to read complex and detailed technical articles, books, and reports; to write technical reports; and to present those reports to groups of people when required. Many schools offer shop classes in electronics and in diagram and blueprint reading.

Postsecondary Training
Avionics engineers must have a bachelor's degree from an accredited college or university and may participate in a cooperative education program through their engineering school. Avionics technicians must have completed a course of training at a postsecondary technical

institute or community college. The training should include at least one year of electronics technician training. If not trained specifically in avionics, students should obtain a solid background in electronics theory and practice. Further specialized training will be done on the job, where technicians work with engineers and senior technicians until they are competent to work without direct supervision.

Larger corporations in the aerospace industry operate their own schools and training institutes. Such training rarely includes theoretical or general studies but concentrates on areas important to the company's functions. The U.S. armed forces also conduct excellent electronics and avionics training schools; their graduates are in high demand in the industry after they leave the service.

Certification or Licensing

All states require engineers to be licensed. There are two levels of licensing for engineers. Professional Engineers (PEs) have graduated from an accredited engineering curriculum, have four years of engineering experience, and have passed a written exam. Engineering graduates need not wait until they have four years experience, however, to start the licensure process. Those who pass the Fundamentals of Engineering examination after graduating are called Engineers in Training (EITs) or Engineer Interns or Intern Engineers. The EIT certification is usually valid for 10 years. After acquiring suitable work experience, EITs can take the second examination, the Principles and Practice of Engineering, to gain full PE licensure.

In order to ensure that avionics engineers are kept up to date on their quickly changing field, many states have imposed continuing education requirements for relicensure.

Federal Communications Commission (FCC) regulations require that anyone who works with radio transmitting equipment have a restricted radiotelephone operator's license. Such a license is issued upon application to the FCC and is issued for life.

Other Requirements

To be successful in this work, you should have strong science and mathematics skills. In addition, you will need to have good manual dexterity and mechanical aptitude and the temperament for exacting work.

EXPLORING

One good way to learn more about avionics is to visit factories and test facilities where avionics technicians work as part of teams designing and testing new equipment. It is also possible to visit a large airfield's repair facilities where avionics technicians inspect, maintain, and calibrate communications and control apparatus. You can also arrange to visit other types of electronics manufacturers.

Useful information about avionics training programs and career opportunities is available from the U.S. armed forces as well as from trade and technical schools and community colleges that offer such programs. These organizations are always pleased to answer inquiries from prospective students or service personnel.

EMPLOYERS

Nearly 60 percent of the 76,000 aerospace engineers employed in the United States work in the aerospace product and parts manufacturing industries. About 10 percent are employed in federal government agencies, primarily the Department of Defense and the National Aeronautics and Space Administration (NASA). Other employers include engineering and architectural services, research and testing services, and search and navigation equipment firms.

There are approximately 22,500 avionics technicians employed in the United States. Most technicians work for airlines or airports and flying fields. Other major employers include the federal government (including NASA) and aircraft assembly firms.

STARTING OUT

Those entering the field of avionics must first obtain the necessary training in electronics. Following that training, the school's career services department can help locate prospective employers, arrange interviews, and advise about an employment search. Other possibilities are to contact an employment agency or to approach a prospective employer directly. Service in the military is an excellent way to gain education, training, and experience in avionics; many companies are eager to hire technicians with a military background.

ADVANCEMENT

Avionics technicians usually begin their careers in trainee positions until they are thoroughly familiar with the requirements and routines of their work. Having completed their apprenticeships, they are usually assigned to work independently, with only minimal supervision, doing testing and repair work. The most experienced and able technicians go on to install new equipment and to work in research and development operations. Many senior technicians move into training, supervisory, sales, and customer relations positions. Some choose to pursue additional training and become avionics engineers.

Avionics engineers are already at an advanced position but may move up to become engineering supervisors or managers.

EARNINGS

The U.S. Department of Labor reports that median annual earnings of aerospace engineers (the category under which the department classifies avionics engineers) were $84,090 in 2005. Salaries ranged from less than $57,250 to more than $117,680. Median annual earnings of engineers who worked for the federal government were $93,050. Engineers who worked in the aerospace product and parts manufacturing industry earned mean salaries of $80,920 in 2005; those employed in electronic instrument manufacturing had mean earnings of $90,630.

Avionics technicians had median earnings of $46,630 in 2005, according to the U.S. Department of Labor. The top 10 percent of technicians earned more than $60,800 a year. The lowest 10 percent earned less than $34,620 a year. Federal government employees (not including armed forces personnel) on the average earn slightly less than avionics technicians employed by private aerospace firms. Their jobs, however, are more secure.

WORK ENVIRONMENT

Avionics engineers and technicians work for aircraft and aerospace manufacturers, airlines, and NASA and other government agencies. Most avionics engineers and technicians specialize in a specific area of avionics; they are also responsible for keeping up with the latest technological and industry advances. Their work is usually performed in pleasant indoor surroundings. Because this work is very precise, successful engineers and technicians must have a personality suited to meeting exact standards and working within small tolerances. Technicians sometimes work in closely cooperating teams. This requires an ability to work with a team spirit of coordinated effort.

OUTLOOK

The U.S. Department of Labor predicts that employment for avionics engineers will grow more slowly than the average for all occupations through 2014. Employment for avionics technicians is expected to grow about as fast as the average during this same time span.

The aerospace industry is closely tied to government spending and to political change, as well as to the economy, which also affects the aircraft and airline industries strongly. The decline in airline travel as a result of the terrorist attacks of September 11, 2001, has led to reduced employment opportunities for avionics engineers and technicians. Opportunities will be better for engineers and technicians employed in military and other government-related aerospace projects.

Despite predictions of slower employment growth, avionics is an important and constantly developing field for which more and more trained engineers and technicians will be required. Reliance on electronic technology has grown rapidly and in virtually every industry. Many defense contractors have begun to branch out into other products, especially in the areas of electronic and computer technology. Commercial applications of the space program, including the launching of privately owned satellites, are also providing new opportunities in the aerospace industry.

FOR MORE INFORMATION

For a list of accredited schools and colleges, contact
Accreditation Board for Engineering and Technology
111 Market Place, Suite 1050
Baltimore, MD 21202-7116
Tel: 410-347-7700
http://www.abet.org

Contact the AIA for publications with information on aerospace technologies, careers, and space.
Aerospace Industries Association (AIA)
1000 Wilson Boulevard, Suite 1700
Arlington, VA 22209-3928
Tel: 703-358-1000
http://www.aia-aerospace.org

For career information and details on student branches of this organization, contact
American Institute of Aeronautics and Astronautics
1801 Alexander Bell Drive, Suite 500
Reston, VA 20191-4344
Tel: 800-639-2422
http://www.aiaa.org

For information on educational programs and to purchase a copy of Engineering: Go For It, *contact*

American Society for Engineering Education
1818 N Street, NW, Suite 600
Washington, DC 20036-2479
Tel: 202-331-3500
http://www.asee.org

For information on general aviation, contact
General Aviation Manufacturers Association
1400 K Street, NW, Suite 801
Washington, DC 20005-2402
Tel: 202-393-1500
http://www.generalaviation.org

For information on careers and student competitions, contact
Junior Engineering Technical Society
1420 King Street, Suite 405
Alexandria, VA 22314-2794
Tel: 703-548-5387
Email: info@jets.org
http://www.jets.org

For career and licensing information, contact
National Society of Professional Engineers
1420 King Street
Alexandria, VA 22314-2794
Tel: 703-684-2800
http://www.nspe.org/students

For career information, see the AIAC's Web site.
Aerospace Industries Association of Canada (AIAC)
60 Queen Street, #1200
Ottawa, ON K1P 5Y7 Canada
Tel: 613-232-4297
Email: info@aiac.ca
http://www.aiac.ca

Chemical Engineers

OVERVIEW

Chemical engineers take chemistry out of the laboratory and into the real world. They are involved in evaluating methods and equipment for the mass production of chemicals and other materials requiring chemical processing. They also develop products from these materials, such as plastics, metals, gasoline, detergents, pharmaceuticals, and foodstuffs. They develop or improve safe, environmentally sound processes, determine the least costly production method, and formulate the material for easy use and safe, economical transportation. Approximately 31,000 chemical engineers work in the United States. Although only a small number of chemical engineers specialize in aviation and aerospace, they play a key role in the success of these industries.

HISTORY

Chemical engineering, defined in its most general sense as applied chemistry, existed even in early civilizations. Ancient Greeks, for example, distilled alcoholic beverages, as did the Chinese, who by 800 BC had learned to distill alcohol from the fermentation of rice. Aristotle, a fourth-century BC Greek philosopher, wrote about a process for obtaining fresh water by evaporating and condensing water from the sea.

The foundations of modern chemical engineering were laid out during the Renaissance, when experimentation and the questioning of accepted scientific theories became widespread. This period saw the development of many new chemical processes, such as those for producing sulfuric acid (for fertilizers and textile treatment) and alkalies (for soap). The atomic theories of John Dalton and Amedeo Avogadro, developed in the 1800s, supplied the theoretical underpinning for modern chemistry and chemical engineering.

With the advent of large-scale manufacturing in the mid-19th century, modern chemical engineering began to take shape. Chemical manufacturers were soon required to seek out chemists familiar with manufacturing processes. These early chemical engineers were called chemical technicians or industrial chemists. The first course in chemical engineering was taught in 1888 at the Massachusetts Institute of Technology. By 1900, "chemical engineer" had become a widely used job title.

Chemical engineers are employed in increasing numbers to design new and more efficient ways to produce chemicals and chemical by-products. In the United States, they have been especially important in the development of petroleum-based fuels for internal combustion engine-powered vehicles. Their achievements range from the large-scale production of plastics, antibiotics, and synthetic rubbers to the development of high-octane gasoline.

THE JOB

Chemical engineering is one of the four major engineering disciplines (the others are electrical, mechanical, and civil). Because chemical engineers are rigorously trained not only in chemistry but also in physics, mathematics, and other sciences such as biology or geology, they are among the most versatile of all engineers, with many specialties, and they are employed in many industries, including aerospace and aviation. Chemical engineers who are employed by the National Aeronautics and Space Administration (NASA), for example, might focus on next-generation fuel cell research, developing fuel cells that use methanol (which is an alcohol that can be created from CO_2), rather than hydrogen. This new type of fuel could be made to power robots and other electrical equipment on Mars, which has CO_2 in its atmosphere. NASA also believes that its chemical engineers might even be able to eventually convert the CO_2 that humans exhale into fuel for its robots, spacecraft, and equipment.

Other chemical engineers employed by NASA or private aviation and aerospace companies might develop new polymers (plastics) for space applications (such as protective coating to shield instrumentation), fine-tune propellant technology and processes, assess the flammability of a new type of fuel that is in development, analyze soil samples from moons or planets to assess their effect on equipment and the health of astronauts, or develop lubricants for spacecrafts that hold up to the extreme conditions of takeoff, space flight, and reentry into the Earth's atmosphere.

There are many stages in the production of chemicals and related materials, and the following paragraphs describe specific jobs responsibilities by production stage for chemical engineers. At smaller companies, engineers may have a hand in all of these production phases, while job duties are more specialized in larger plants.

Research engineers work with chemists to develop new processes and products, or they may develop better methods to make existing products. Product ideas may originate with the company's marketing department; with a chemist, chemical engineer, or other specialist; or with a customer. The basic chemical process for the product is then developed in a laboratory, where various experiments are conducted to determine the process's viability. Some projects die here.

Others go on to be developed and refined at pilot plants, which are small-scale versions of commercial plants. Chemical engineers in these plants run tests on the processes and make any necessary modifications. They strive to improve the process, reduce safety hazards and waste, and cut production time and costs. Throughout the development stage, engineers keep detailed records of the proceedings, and they may abandon projects that aren't viable.

When a new process is judged to be viable, *process design engineers* determine how the product can most efficiently be produced on a large scale while still guaranteeing a consistently high-quality result. These engineers consider process requirements and cost, convenience and safety for the operators, waste minimization, legal regulations, and preservation of the environment. Besides working on the steps of the process, they also work on the design of the equipment to be used in the process. These chemical engineers are often assisted in plant and equipment design by mechanical, electrical, and civil engineers.

Project engineers oversee the construction of new plants and installation of new equipment. In construction, chemical engineers may work as *field engineers,* who are involved in the testing and initial operation of the equipment and assist in plant start-up and operator training. Once a process is fully implemented at a manufacturing plant, *production engineers* supervise the day-to-day operations. They are responsible for the rate of production, scheduling, worker safety, quality control, and other important operational concerns.

Chemical engineers working in environmental control are involved in waste management, recycling, and control of air and water pollution. They work with the engineers in research and development, process design, equipment and plant construction, and production to incorporate environmental protection measures into all stages of the chemical engineering process.

As *technical sales engineers,* chemical engineers may work with customers of manufactured products to determine what best fits their needs. They answer questions such as "Could our products be used more economically than those now in use? Why does this paint peel?" etc. Others work as managers, making policy and business decisions and overseeing the training of new personnel. The variety of job descriptions is almost limitless because of chemical engineers' versatility and adaptability.

REQUIREMENTS

High School
High school students interested in chemical engineering should take all the mathematics and science courses their schools offer. These should include algebra, geometry, calculus, trigonometry, chemistry, physics, and biology. Computer science courses are also highly recommended. In addition, students should take four years of English, and a foreign language is valuable. To enhance their desirability, students should participate in high school science and engineering clubs and other extracurricular activities.

Postsecondary Training
A bachelor's degree in chemical engineering is the minimum educational requirement for entering the field. For some positions, an M.S., an M.B.A., or a Ph.D. may be required. A Ph.D. may be essential for advancement in research, teaching, and administration.

For their college studies, students should attend a chemical engineering program approved by the Accreditation Board for Engineering and Technology and the American Institute of Chemical Engineers (AIChE). There are more than 150 accredited undergraduate programs in chemical engineering in the United States offering bachelor's degrees. Some engineering programs last five or six years; these often include work experience in industry.

As career plans develop, students should consult with advisors about special career paths in which they are interested. Those who want to teach or conduct research will need a graduate degree. There are approximately 140 accredited chemical engineering graduate programs in the United States. A master's degree generally takes two years of study beyond undergraduate school, while a Ph.D. program requires four to six years.

In graduate school, students specialize in one aspect of chemical engineering, such as chemical kinetics or biotechnology. Graduate education also helps to obtain promotions, and some companies offer tuition reimbursement to encourage employees to take graduate courses. For engineers who would like to become managers, a master's degree in business administration may be helpful. Chemical engineers must be prepared for a lifetime of education to keep up with rapid advances in technology.

Certification or Licensing
Chemical engineers must be licensed as professional engineers if their work involves providing services directly to the public. All 50 states and the District of Columbia have specific licensing requirements, which include graduation from an accredited engineering school, passing a written exam, and having at least four years of engineering experience. About one-third of all chemical engineers are licensed; they are called registered engineers.

Other Requirements
Important personal qualities are honesty, accuracy, objectivity, and perseverance. In addition, chemical engineers must be inquisitive, open minded, creative, and flexible. Problem-solving ability is essential. To remain competitive in the job market, they should display initiative and leadership skills, exhibit the ability to work well in teams and collaborate across disciplines, and be able to work with people of different linguistic and cultural backgrounds.

EXPLORING
High school students should join science clubs and take part in other extracurricular activities and join such organizations as the Junior Engineering Technical Society (JETS). JETS participants have opportunities to enter engineering design and problem-solving contests and to learn team development skills. Science contests are also a good way to apply principles learned in classes to a special project. Students can also subscribe to the American Chemical Society's *Chem Matters*, a quarterly magazine for high school chemistry students.

College students can join professional associations, such as the American Chemical Society (ACS), AIChE, and the Society of Manufacturing Engineers (composed of individual associations with specific fields of interest), as student affiliates. Membership benefits include subscriptions to magazines—some of them geared specifically toward students—that provide the latest industry information. College students can also contact ACS or AIChE local sections to arrange to talk with some chemical engineers about what they do. These associations can also help them find summer or co-op work experiences.

In addition, the Society of Women Engineers (SWE) has a mentor program in which high school and college women are matched with an SWE member in their area. This member is available to answer questions and provide a firsthand introduction to a career in engineering.

EMPLOYERS

There are approximately 31,000 chemical engineers working in the United States. While many chemical engineers work in manufacturing industries, others are employed by federal and state governments, colleges and universities, and research and testing services. The list of individual employers, if cited, would take many pages. However, the following industry classifications indicate where most chemical engineers are employed: aerospace, fuels, electronics, food and consumer products, design and construction, materials, biotechnology, pharmaceuticals, environmental control, pulp and paper, public utilities, and consultation firms. Because of the nature of their training and background, chemical engineers can easily obtain employment with another company in a completely different field if necessary or desired.

STARTING OUT

Most chemical engineers obtain their first position through company recruiters sent to college campuses. Others may find employment with companies with whom they have had summer or work-study arrangements. Many respond to advertisements in professional journals or newspapers. The Internet now offers multiple opportunities to job seekers, and many libraries have programs that offer assistance in making use of the available job listings. Chemical engineers may also contact colleges and universities regarding positions as part-time teaching or laboratory assistants if they wish to continue study for a graduate degree. Student members of professional societies often use the employment services of these organizations, including resume data banks, online job listings, national employment clearinghouses, and employers' mailing lists. Job seekers who wish to work for NASA should visit http://www.nasajobs.nasa.gov for more information on available positions. If they are interested in working for aviation and aerospace companies, they should visit company Web sites to learn more about career options.

Typically, new recruits begin as trainees or process engineers. They often begin work under the supervision of seasoned engineers. Many participate in special training programs designed to orient them to company processes, procedures, policies, and products. This allows the company to determine where the new personnel may best fulfill their needs. After this training period, new employees often rotate positions to get an all-around experience in working for the company.

ADVANCEMENT

Entry-level personnel usually advance to project or production engineers after learning the ropes in product manufacturing. They may then be assigned to sales and marketing. A large percentage of engineers no longer do engineering work by the tenth year of their employment. At that point, they often advance to supervisory or management positions. An M.B.A. enhances their opportunities for promotion. A doctoral degree is essential for university teaching or supervisory research positions. Some engineers may decide at this point that they prefer to start their own consulting firms. Continued advancement, raises, and increased responsibility are not automatic but depend on sustained demonstration of leadership skills.

EARNINGS

Though starting salaries have dipped somewhat in recent years, chemical engineering is still one of the highest-paid scientific professions. Salaries vary with education, experience, industry, and employer. The U.S. Department of Labor reports that the median annual salary for chemical engineers was $77,140 in 2005. The lowest-paid 10 percent earned less than $49,350; the highest-paid 10 percent earned more than $113,950 annually. According to a 2005 salary survey by the National Association of Colleges and Employers, starting annual salaries for those with bachelor's degrees in chemical engineering averaged $53,813; with master's degrees, $57,260; and Ph.Ds, $79,591. Chemical engineers with doctoral degrees and many years of experience in supervisory and management positions may have salaries exceeding $100,000 annually. Engineers employed by NASA earned starting salaries that ranged from $33,151 to $44,034 in 2006.

Benefits offered depend on the employer; however, chemical engineers typically receive such things as paid vacation and sick days, health insurance, and retirement plans.

WORK ENVIRONMENT

Because the industries in which chemical engineers work are so varied—from academia to waste treatment and disposal—the working conditions also vary. Most chemical engineers work in clean, well-maintained offices, laboratories, or plants, although some occasionally work outdoors, particularly construction engineers. Travel to new or existing plants may be required. Some chemical engineers work with dangerous chemicals, but the adoption of safe working practices has greatly reduced potential health hazards. Chemical engineers at institutions of higher learning spend their time in classrooms or research laboratories.

The workweek for a chemical engineer in manufacturing is usually 40 hours, although many work longer hours. Because plants often operate around the clock, they may work different shifts or have irregular hours.

OUTLOOK

The U.S. Department of Labor projects that employment for chemical engineers will grow about as fast as the average for all occupations through 2014. Certain areas of the field will offer more job opportunities than others. Chemical and pharmaceutical companies, for example, will need engineers in research and development to work on new chemicals and more efficient processes. Additionally, growth will come in service industries, such as companies providing research and testing services. Job opportunities will be best in the energy, biotechnology, and nanotechnology segments of this industry sector.

Slower-than-average employment growth is expected through 2014 in aerospace product and parts manufacturing and related industries. Despite this prediction, the expertise of chemical engineers will continue to be needed by this industry. Engineers who have advanced degrees and experience in the aerospace and aviation industries will enjoy the best employment opportunities.

FOR MORE INFORMATION

Contact the AIA for publications with information on aerospace technologies, careers, and space.
   Aerospace Industries Association (AIA)
   1000 Wilson Boulevard, Suite 1700
   Arlington, VA 22209-3928

Tel: 703-358-1000
http://www.aia-aerospace.org

For information on undergraduate internships, summer jobs, and co-op programs, contact
American Chemical Society
1155 16th Street, NW
Washington, DC 20036-4801
Tel: 800-227-5558
Email: help@acs.org
http://www.chemistry.org

For career information and information on student branches of this organization, contact the AIAA.
American Institute of Aeronautics and Astronautics (AIAA)
1801 Alexander Bell Drive, Suite 500
Reston, VA 20191-4344
Tel: 800-639-2422
http://www.aiaa.org

For information on awards, accredited programs, internships, student chapters, and career opportunities, contact
American Institute of Chemical Engineers
3 Park Avenue
New York, NY 10016-5991
Tel: 800-242-4363
http://www.aiche.org

For information about programs, products, and a chemical engineering career brochure, contact
Junior Engineering Technical Society
1420 King Street, Suite 405
Alexandria, VA 22314-2750
Tel: 703-548-5387
Email: info@jets.org
http://www.jets.org

For information on aeronautical careers, internships, and student projects, visit NASA's Web site.
National Aeronautics and Space Administration (NASA)
Public Communications and Inquiries Management Office
Suite 1M32
Washington, DC 20546-0001

Tel: 202-358-0001
Email: public-inquiries@hq.nasa.gov
http://www.nasa.gov

For information on National Engineers Week Programs held in many U.S. locations, contact
National Engineers Week Headquarters
1420 King Street
Alexandria, VA 22314-2750
Tel: 703-684-2852
Email: eweek@nspe.org
http://www.eweek.org

For information on training programs, seminars, and how to become a student member, contact
Society of Manufacturing Engineers
One SME Drive
Dearborn, MI 48121-2408
Tel: 800-733-4763
Email: careermentor@sme.org
http://www.sme.org

For information on career guidance literature, scholarships, and mentor programs, contact
Society of Women Engineers
230 East Ohio Street, Suite 400
Chicago, IL 60611-3265
Tel: 312-596-5223
Email: hq@swe.org
http://www.swe.org

College Professors, Aerospace/Aviation

OVERVIEW

Aerospace/aviation professors teach students about aerospace, aviation science, or related fields of study at colleges and universities. Primarily, they give classroom instruction but may also be assigned to conduct departmental research or provide educational guidance to students. Others may work as flight instructors, teaching students how to fly aircraft. Many choose academia after a successful career as an engineer, scientist, or pilot. There are approximately 8,800 postsecondary atmospheric, earth, marine, and space sciences teachers and about 109,000 flight instructors working in the United States.

HISTORY

The aerospace industry was born in the early part of the 20th century and literally took off shortly after Orville and Wilbur Wright's first flight in 1903. Orville made the first flight, flying their wood, wire, and cloth airplane 120 feet. What had begun as a curiosity gathered intense interest as pilots and inventors worked to improve the Wright brothers' design. By 1911, airplanes were being used in war. The recognition of the value of aircraft for warfare led to intense efforts to develop the aerospace industry, and technological advances in aviation design developed at an incredible pace. In 1915, the aerospace industry in the United States was stimulated by the creation of the National Advisory Committee for

Aeronautics, which would later become the National Aeronautics and Space Administration (NASA) in 1958.

The beginnings of astronautics, which later would become NASA's focus, followed closely on the heels of the airplane in the early part of the 20th century. Astronautics, the science of space flight, soon revolutionized not only modern warfare but also humanity's vision of its place in the universe.

Today, the United States and Russia are world leaders in space exploration. These countries, in cooperation with 14 other nations, have combined technology and manpower to build, expand, and maintain an international space station. The International Space Station has become the largest, most sophisticated, and most powerful spacecraft ever built.

These achievements would not have been possible without college teachers who have trained future space scientists, engineers, technicians, pilots, managers, and other professionals. Today, hundreds of colleges and universities offer space-related programs or coursework. The University Aviation Association promotes the advancement of degree-granting aviation programs. It has more than 800 institutional members, including 115 colleges and universities.

THE JOB

The aerospace industry is a very diverse field, ranging from defense systems and weapons, to powerful telescopes and other data-gathering technology, to satellite technology, to spacecraft and exploration vehicles, to the science that supports human space flight and exploration. Individuals well trained in a variety of disciplines are in constant demand to work for private aerospace corporations, engineering companies, and aeronautical manufacturers, as well as government agencies such as NASA.

Aerospace/aviation professors teach students interested in pursuing careers in the aerospace and aviation industries. They teach at colleges and universities throughout the United States. Professors have backgrounds in many different disciplines—including most engineering specialties such as mechanical, aerospace, civil, electrical, and computer; mathematics; physics; the biological sciences; and many other fields. Some people turn to teaching after a successful career as an engineer, mathematician, or scientist.

Most aerospace professors have a Ph.D. in their specialty. While some two-year schools may hire professors with a master's degree, most if not all colleges granting four-year degrees desire their professors to have advanced degrees.

The main responsibility of aerospace/aviation professors is to provide education and training to students. Professors teach anywhere from one three-hour course to a full class load per semester. They conduct research, prepare class lectures and examinations, and grade papers and projects. Professors often supervise laboratory-based learning where students can apply their classroom education to hands-on experiments. Classes taught by aerospace/aviation professors at the undergraduate level might include Introduction to Aerospace Engineering, Introduction to Astronomy, Astrodynamics, and Advanced Flight Structures.

Aerospace/aviation professors also serve as advisors or guidance counselors to students assigned to them by their department. In this capacity, professors listen to students' problems and suggest solutions, offer career advice and direction, or perhaps assist them in finding summer employment or an internship. They may make use of their contacts at Boeing, for example, to give a promising student an edge for a highly competitive internship. Aerospace/aviation professors often recruit and guide top students to work for pet projects or departmental research.

Publication in an industry journal is also a feather in any professor's hat. In fact, a published article or research project is often necessary to obtain tenure.

In order to stay current with changing technology and advances in aerospace science, professors often consult with industry professionals, read industry publications, and pursue continuing education. NASA, for example, offers a Summer Faculty Fellowship designed specifically for engineering and science educators teaching at U.S. colleges and universities. Those selected for the fellowship spend time at NASA's Space Flight Center, conducting research on topics such as the use of microgravity to improve fiber optics or honing their teaching skills relating to computer and video systems. In addition, professors attend weekly seminars, participate with NASA colleagues in an exchange of ideas and proposals, and learn fresh ways to teach classroom materials.

Flight instructors are pilots who use their experience, knowledge, joy of flying, and ability to explain complex subjects to teach students how to fly aircraft. Flight instructors give classroom as well as hands-on flying instruction to their students. Topics covered include aerodynamics, navigation, instrument reading, aircraft control techniques, and federal aviation regulations. They may teach at flight schools, for airlines, or in the military or work as self-employed instructors. Flight instructors enter the field after careers as commercial or military pilots. Some choose to hold corporate or federal employment while teaching.

REQUIREMENTS
High School
Your high school's college preparatory program likely includes courses in English, science, math, and physics. In addition, you should take courses in speech to get a sense of what it will be like to lecture to a group of students. Your school's debate team can also help you develop public speaking skills, along with research skills.

Postsecondary Training
At least one advanced degree in your field of study (such as engineering, mathematics, astrobiology, or astrophysics) is required to be a professor in a college or university. The master's degree is considered the minimum standard, and graduate work beyond the master's is usually desirable. If you hope to advance in academic rank above instructor, most institutions require a doctorate.

In the last year of your undergraduate program, you'll apply to graduate programs in your area of study. Standards for admission to a graduate program can be high and the competition heavy, depending on the school. Once accepted into a program, your responsibilities will be similar to those of your professors—in addition to attending seminars, you'll research, prepare articles for publication, and teach some undergraduate courses.

You may find employment in a junior college with only a master's degree. Advancement in responsibility and in salary, however, is more likely to come if you have earned a doctorate.

Although the Federal Aviation Administration (FAA) does not require flight instructors to have a particular degree, a college education is highly recommended. You may want to attend a university with a specialized aviation program, such as the Institute of Aviation at the University of Illinois-Urbana Champaign. Another option is to get your pilot training in the military; contact your local recruiting offices for more information. If you do not attend a specialized aviation program or get your training in the military, you will need to get flight instruction, either from an instructor who offers private lessons or through a flight school, also known as pilot school. The FAA provides information on pilot schools; visit http://www.faa.gov to find out more.

Certification and Licensing
No certification or licensing is available for aerospace/aviation professors.

To become a flight instructor, you will need to get FAA flight instructor certification. To do this, you must have a commercial pilot's certification for the kind of aircraft (single engine, multiengine, instrument, etc.) that matches the flight instructor rating (designation) you want to have. You must have accumulated a certain amount of flying time and have your logbook properly endorsed. You must have completed training that covered topics such as evaluation of student flight performance, lesson planning, and how to properly instruct on stall awareness, spin entry, spins, and spin recovery methods. In addition, you will need to pass a test with written and oral sections as well as a flight test. Certification renewal is on a two-year basis.

The National Association of Flight Instructors offers several professional certifications, including the master certificated flight instructor and the master certificated flight instructor-aerobatic. These certifications are voluntary and demonstrate commitment to the profession. To earn these, an instructor must meet certain requirements, such as being a member of the association, having FAA flight instructor certification, and completing a certain amount of continuing education credits or activities.

Other Requirements

College professors should enjoy reading, writing, and researching. Not only will you spend many years studying in school, but your whole career will be based on communicating your thoughts and ideas. People skills are important because you'll be dealing directly with students, administrators, and other faculty members on a daily basis. You should feel comfortable in a role of authority and possess self-confidence.

If you work as a flight instructor, you must pass a physical exam and be certified fit to fly. Naturally, anyone controlling an aircraft needs to have good vision, so you must have eyesight of 20/20 or better in each eye, although you can wear glasses or contact lenses to get this. Good hearing is also a requirement. In addition to physical and intellectual requirements, flight instructors need to be calm, have good judgment, be able to deal well with people, and—of course—have the "flying bug."

EXPLORING

Your high school teachers use many of the same skills as college professors, so talk to them about their careers and their college experiences. You can develop your own teaching experience by volunteering at a community center, working at a day care center, or working at a summer camp. Also, spend some time on a college campus to get a sense of the environment. Write to colleges for their admissions brochures and course catalogs (or check them out online); read about the faculty members and the courses they teach. Before visiting college campuses, make arrangements to speak to professors who teach courses that interest you. These professors may allow you to sit in on their classes and observe. Also, make appointments with college advisers and with people in the admissions and recruitment offices. If your grades are good enough, you might be able to serve as a teaching assistant during your undergraduate years, which can give you experience leading discussions and grading papers.

EMPLOYERS

Approximately 8,800 postsecondary atmospheric, earth, marine, and space sciences teachers and about 109,000 flight instructors are employed in the United States. Employment opportunities vary based on area of study and education. With a doctorate, a number of publications, and a record of good teaching, professors should find opportunities in universities across the country. There are more than 3,800 colleges and universities in the United States; many offer aerospace- and aviation-related programs and coursework. Professors teach in undergraduate and graduate programs. The teaching jobs at doctoral institutions are usually better paying and more prestigious. The most sought-after positions offer tenure. Teachers that have only a master's degree will be limited to opportunities with junior colleges, community colleges, and some small private institutions.

Flight instructors in the military are employed by the U. S. government. In the civilian world, flight instructors are typically employed by flight schools or they may work independently, offering lessons on their own. Some instructors may begin by working at an established flight school but have the goal of eventually running their own school. Flight schools are located all across the country, and many airports have them.

STARTING OUT

You should start the process of finding a teaching position while you are in graduate school. The process includes developing a curriculum vitae (a detailed, academic resume), writing for publication, assisting with research, attending conferences, and gaining teaching experience and recommendations. Many students begin applying for teaching positions while finishing their graduate program. For most positions at four-year institutions, you must travel to large conferences where interviews can be arranged with representatives from the universities to which you have applied.

Because of the competition for tenure-track positions, you may have to work for a few years in temporary positions, visiting various schools as an *adjunct professor*. Some professional associations maintain lists of teaching opportunities in their areas. They may also make lists of applicants available to college administrators looking to fill an available position.

Some flight instructors start out with careers as military pilots then become instructors later in their professional lives. Another way to gain entry into the field is through connections made at flight school. In fact, students who have impressed their instructors may be offered a job there.

ADVANCEMENT

The normal pattern of advancement is from instructor to assistant professor, to associate professor, to full professor. All four academic ranks are concerned primarily with teaching and research. College faculty members who have an interest in and a talent for administration may be advanced to chair of a department or to dean of their college. A few become college or university presidents or other types of administrators.

The instructor is usually an inexperienced college teacher. He or she may hold a doctorate or may have completed all the Ph.D. requirements except for the dissertation. Most colleges look upon the rank of instructor as the period during which the college is trying out the teacher. Instructors usually are advanced to the position of assistant professors within three to four years. Assistant professors are given up to about six years to prove themselves worthy of tenure, and if they do so, they become associate professors. Some professors choose to remain at the associate level. Others strive to become full professors and receive greater status, salary, and responsibilities.

Most colleges have clearly defined promotion policies from rank to rank for faculty members, and many have written statements about the number of years in which instructors and assistant professors may remain in grade. Administrators in many colleges hope to encourage younger faculty members to increase their skills and competencies and thus to qualify for the more demanding positions of associate professor and full professor.

Advancement for flight instructors often depends on the individual's goals. Some instructors may want to advance to the point of running their own schools. An instructor working at a small airport school may want to move on to work at a large school in a metropolitan area or at a school that is part of a university. And other instructors may simply want to increase the number of students they teach. No matter what the goal, however, the best way to make any type of advancement in this field is by gaining as much personal flying experience as possible and becoming certified to pilot a variety of aircraft.

EARNINGS

Earnings vary by the departments professors work in, by the size of the school, by the type of school (public, private, women's only, for example), and by the level of position the professor holds. In its 2004-05 salary survey, the American Association of University Professors (AAUP) reported the average yearly income for all full-time faculty was $68,505. It also reports that professors averaged the following salaries by rank: full professors, $91,548; associate professors, $65,113; assistant professors, $54,571; instructors, $39,899; and lecturers, $45,647. According to the U.S. Department of Labor, in 2004, the median salary for postsecondary atmospheric, Earth, marine, and space sciences teachers was $65,720 in 2005, with 10 percent earning $115,270 or more and 10 percent earning $35,240 or less.

Many professors try to increase their earnings by completing research, publishing in their field, or teaching additional courses. Professors working on the West Coast and the East Coast and those working at doctorate-granting institutions tend to have the highest salaries.

Flight instructors' earnings vary based on factors such as the size and type of employer, the type of aircraft used, and the amount of experience the instructor has. According to the FAA, instructors working at flight schools may earn from $12,300 to $40,530 a year. A few flight instructors with extensive experience that work for major airlines may earn as much as $75,000 or more a year. Instructors who work independently (that is, are self-employed) typically charge an hourly fee, which may be approximately between $30 and $50 an hour. Their yearly income, though, depends on the number of students they have and the amount of time they are actually able to spend teaching.

Benefits for full-time faculty typically include health insurance and retirement funds and, in some cases, stipends for travel related to research, housing allowances, and tuition waivers for dependents.

WORK ENVIRONMENT

A college or university is usually a pleasant place in which to work. Campuses bustle with all types of activities and events, stimulating ideas, and a young, energetic population. Much prestige comes with success as a professor and scholar; professors have the respect of students, colleagues, and others in their community.

Depending on the size of the department, aerospace/aviation teachers may have their own office, or they may have to share an office with one or more colleagues. Their department may provide them with a computer, Internet access, and research assistants. College professors are also able to do much of their office work at home. They can arrange their schedule around class hours, academic meetings, and the established office hours when they meet with students. Most aerospace/aviation teachers work more than 40 hours each week. Although college professors may teach only two or three classes a semester, they spend many hours preparing for lectures, examining student work, and conducting research.

Flight instructors work in classrooms and in aircraft, and they must be comfortable working with computers, machines, and people. In order to accommodate their students' schedules, many instructors hold classes in the evenings or on weekends. FAA rules limit the number of hours per day that a flight instructor can spend giving in-flight instruction; however, instructors can spend as much time as they want doing classroom work. On average, instructors work between 40 and 50 hours a week. Those who work at small schools or independently may spend part of their time teaching and part of their time doing other flying jobs to supplement their income.

OUTLOOK

The U.S. Department of Labor predicts much faster-than-average employment growth for college and university professors through 2014. College enrollment is projected to grow due to an increased number of 18- to 24-year-olds, an increased number of adults returning to college, and an increased number of foreign-born students. Although employment in aerospace products and parts manufacturing is expected to grow more slowly than the average, well-trained workers will always be needed in this multi-billion-dollar industry. Additionally, opportunities for college teachers will be good in areas such as engineering and computer science, which offer strong career prospects in the aerospace and aviation industries. Retirement of current faculty members will also provide job openings. However, competition for full-time, tenure-track positions at four-year schools will be very strong.

FOR MORE INFORMATION

To read about the issues affecting college professors, contact the following organizations:

American Association of University Professors
1012 14th Street, NW, Suite 500
Washington, DC 20005-3406
Tel: 202-737-5900
Email: aaup@aaup.org
http://www.aaup.org

American Federation of Teachers
555 New Jersey Avenue, NW
Washington, DC 20001-2029
Tel: 202-879-4400
Email: online@aft.org
http://www.aft.org

For information on professional certifications, contact
National Association of Flight Instructors
EAA Aviation Center
PO Box 3086
Oshkosh, WI 54903-3086
Tel: 920-426-6801
http://www.NAFInet.org

For information on aviation education and camps, visit the following Web site:
National Coalition for Aviation Education
http://www.aviationeducation.org

For information on postsecondary aviation programs, contact
University Aviation Association
3410 Skyway Drive
Auburn, AL 36830-6444
Tel: 334-844-2434
Email: uaa@auburn.edu
http://www.uaa.aero

INTERVIEW

Dr. Shan de Silva is professor and chairperson in the Department of Space Studies of the John D. Odegard School of Aerospace Sciences (http://www.space.edu/aerospace/home.php) at the University of North Dakota. He discussed his career and the education of aerospace students with the editors of Careers in Focus: Space Exploration.

Q. Please tell us about yourself and your professional background.

A. I am currently professor and chairperson in the Department of Space Studies at the University of North Dakota. I am also director of the North Dakota Space Grant Consortium and the North Dakota NASA ESPCoR Program. In these roles I am responsible for developing a space education and research infrastructure in the state of North Dakota.

I am a geologist by training with a research focus in volcanology and remote sensing. I completed my Ph.D. in 1987 and then spent three years at the Lunar and Planetary Institute as a visiting scientist. Before I came to North Dakota, I spent 11 years at Indiana State University teaching geology and astronomy courses and managing the faculty computing resource center.

Q. What made you want to become a space studies educator?

A. Space exploration is inherently exciting and is a great vehicle through which we can develop interdisciplinary education programs. To understand space exploration, a student must understand the interplay among science, technical, humanities, political, and the business side of knowledge. The industry is full of workers who are deeply trained in their disciplines, yet they work in an interdisciplinary enterprise. Developing and providing educational programs that allow people to develop their interdisciplinary understanding while paying attention to disciplinary depth is challenging and exciting. Space studies demands such an approach, and it is the wave of future.

Q. Tell us about the space studies program at the university.

A. Currently, students may attain a master of science in space studies either on campus or online through our distance degree program. We have about 120 students active at any one time. Our distance program is among the leaders in the use of technology to enhance the learning experience, with over 500 graduates benefiting from interactivity and real-time communication between students and professors. Individual research is emphasized both on campus and at distance. Undergraduate students may also pursue a minor in the space studies field. Our programs all emphasize interdisciplinary learning.

Q. For what type of jobs does your program prepare students?
A. Our program goal is to integrate, rather than separate, traditional disciplines related to space. While specialized technical training is an essential part of the space community, the all-encompassing nature of space development also requires people who possess a broader background that links policy, business, law, science, and technology. The Department of Space Studies at the University of North Dakota seeks to prepare this vital segment of the community so that they can become the educators, scientists, engineers, planners, managers, troubleshooters, negotiators, and communicators of the space community. Our graduates are well placed in the aerospace industry, at NASA centers and contractors, at federal agencies, as educators, and in the armed forces.

Q. Can you tell us about the internship opportunities available to students?
A. Internships or experiential learning opportunities are a feature of our on-campus program. For graduate students, these are a part of their research program/project and involve collaborative work with external experts and laboratories (NASA, other federal, or other academic institutions), fieldwork, or work experience as required and arranged with the advisor. For undergraduates, NASA internships and workforce development experience are available through the North Dakota Space Grant Consortium. We also offer a field trip to Russia and hope to develop others to other international venues.

Q. What advice would you offer space studies majors as they graduate and look for jobs?
A. Ensure you have a core expertise in one of the subdisciplines of space studies and develop a strong interdisciplinary understanding of the space enterprise. Be open to all possibilities as

many job openings in this field are nontraditional. The key is to get in the game; once in, the options multiply significantly.

Q. What is the future of your program and space studies in general?

A. The future for our program is bright. This is a unique academic area, and we are the leader in interdisciplinary graduate education in space studies. The level of faculty expertise and curricular rigor is a cornerstone of the program. The accessibility of our program through distance education technologies is unparalleled.

The academic field of space studies will consolidate and grow as our future in space becomes clearer. The need for an interdisciplinary understanding of space will become more of a priority over traditional disciplinary knowledge. We are well positioned to continue our leadership role in this area.

Computer Engineers

OVERVIEW

Computer engineers employed in the aerospace industry work with the computer systems needed to operate sophisticated machinery such as aircraft and spacecraft, robots, defense missiles, and satellites. They may specialize in either software—the programs used to run computers—or hardware—the physical parts of a computer, or work in both specialties. Most computer engineers have a degree in computer science or engineering or an equivalent computer background and knowledge. There are about 877,000 computer engineers employed in the United States; only a small percentage of this total works in the aviation and aerospace industries.

HISTORY

What started as a specialty of electrical engineering has developed into a career field of its own. Today, many individuals interested in a career in one of the computer industry's most promising sectors turn to computer engineering. Computer engineers improve, repair, and implement changes needed to keep up with the demand for faster and stronger computers and complex software programs. Some specialize in the design of the hardware: computer or peripheral parts such as memory chips, motherboards, or microprocessors. Others specialize in creating and organizing information systems for businesses and the government.

THE JOB

Humanity would never have set foot on the moon, launched the space shuttle, built the Hubble Space Telescope, or achieved countless other aerospace milestones without the contributions of computer engineers. These highly trained professionals are key members of interdisciplinary teams at the National Aeronautics and Space Administration (NASA) and private aviation and aerospace companies. There are two main types of computer engineers: *software engineers* and *hardware engineers*.

Software engineers define and analyze specific problems, and help develop computer software applications that effectively solve them. They fall into two basic categories: *systems software engineers* and *applications software engineers*.

Systems software engineers build and maintain entire computer systems for a company or government agency. NASA's X-Ray Astronomy Department, for example, may need a camera to operate at high altitudes while perched on a moving balloon gondola. Systems software engineers suggest ways to coordinate all these parts and design the computer systems that will allow the camera to function and relay information back to NASA headquarters.

Applications software engineers design, create, and modify general computer applications software or specialized utility programs. They might work with astronomers, for example, who receive thousands of pieces of data every hour from probes and satellites in space as well as telescopes here on Earth. If the astronomers had to process the information themselves, compile careful comparisons with previous years' readings, look for patterns or cycles, and keep accurate records of the origin of the various data, it would be so cumbersome and lengthy a project as to make their work next to impossible. They can, however, process the data with the extensive help of computers and software engineers. Applications software engineers define and analyze the challenges of processing this information and help develop computer software applications that effectively resolve these issues. Other applications software engineers might develop software that runs flight simulators or allows scientists to remotely access and control scientific equipment such as the Mars Exploration Rovers.

Computer hardware engineers work with the physical parts of computers, such as CPUs (computer processing units), motherboards, chipsets, video cards, cooling units, magnetic tape, disk drives, storage devices, network cards, and all the components that connect them, down to wires, nuts, and bolts. They are also responsible for all peripheral devices such as printers, scanners, keyboards, modems, and monitors, digital cameras, external storage, and speaker systems, among others. Hardware engineers also design parts and create prototypes using CAD/CAM technology. For example, a hardware engineer employed by Boeing could be assigned to streamline computer monitors to be installed in a new fighter jet. Parts would be redesigned and redeveloped through multiple testing procedures. Once a final design is complete, hardware engineers oversee the manufacture and installation of the monitor.

Both software and hardware engineers must be extremely detail oriented. Software engineers must account for every bit of information accrued by a programming command. Hardware components must often be designed or revised to certain specifications and may change as the project proceeds. Computer engineers often work with other engineers, scientists, and company executives in order to complete a project.

Computer engineers are usually responsible for a significant amount of technical writing, including project proposals, progress reports, and user manuals. They are required to meet regularly with clients and managers to keep project goals clear and learn about any changes as quickly as possible.

REQUIREMENTS

High School
A bachelor's or advanced degree in computer science or engineering is required for most computer engineers. Thus, to prepare for college studies while in high school, take as many computer, math, and science courses as possible; they provide fundamental math and computer knowledge and teach analytical thinking skills. Classes that rely on schematic drawing and flowcharts are also very valuable. English and speech courses will help you improve your communication skills, which are very important for computer engineers.

Postsecondary Training
Computer engineers need at least a bachelor's degree in computer engineering, hardware engineering, software engineering, computer science, or electrical engineering. Employment in research laboratories or academic institutions might require a master's or Ph.D. in computer science or engineering. For a list of accredited four-year computer engineering programs, contact the Accreditation Board for Engineering and Technology (http://www.abet.org).

Obtaining a postsecondary degree in computer engineering is usually considered challenging and even difficult. In addition to natural ability, you should be hard working and determined to succeed. If you plan to work in a specific technical field, such as aviation or aerospace, you should receive some formal training in that particular discipline.

Certification or Licensing

Not all computer professionals are certified. The deciding factor seems to be if it is required by their employer. Many companies offer tuition reimbursement, or incentives, to those who earn certification. Certification is available in a variety of specialties. The Institute for Certification of Computing Professionals offers the associate computing professional designation for those new to the field and the certified computing professional designation for those with at least 48 months of full-time professional-level work in computer-based information systems. Certification is considered by many to be a measure of industry knowledge as well as leverage when negotiating salary.

Other Requirements

Computer engineers need a broad knowledge of and experience with computer systems, software, and technologies. You need strong problem-solving and analysis skills and good interpersonal skills. You must also be detail oriented and work well under pressure. Patience, self-motivation, and flexibility are important. Often, a number of projects are worked on simultaneously, so the ability to multitask is important. Because of rapid technological advances in the computer field, continuing education is a necessity.

EXPLORING

Try to spend a day with a working computer engineer or technician in order to experience firsthand what their job is like. School guidance counselors can help you arrange such a visit. You can also talk to your high school computer teacher for more information.

In general, you should be intent on learning as much as possible about computers and computer software and hardware. You should learn about new developments by reading trade magazines and talking to other computer users. You also can join computer clubs and surf the Internet for information about working in this field.

EMPLOYERS

Approximately 877,000 computer engineers are employed in the United States. About 800,000 work with computer software and 77,000 work with computer hardware. Computer engineering is done in many fields, including aerospace, military, industrial, medical, communications, scientific, and other commercial businesses. Typical aviation and aerospace employers include NASA; the U.S. Department of Defense; the U.S. military; Boeing; Lockheed Martin Corporation; United Technologies Corporation; General Dynamics; Honeywell International Inc.; and Northrop Grumman Corporation.

STARTING OUT

If you have work experience and perhaps even an associate's degree, you may be promoted to a computer engineering technician position from an entry-level job in quality assurance or technical support. Those already employed by computer companies or large corporations should read company job postings to learn about promotion opportunities. If you are already employed and would like to train in computer engineering, either on the job or through formal education, you can investigate future career possibilities within your same company and advise management of your wish to change career tracks. Some companies offer tuition reimbursement for employees who train in areas applicable to business operations.

As a technical, vocational, or university student of computer engineering, you should work closely with your school's career services offices, as many professionals find their first position through on-campus recruiting. Career service office staff are well trained to provide tips on resume writing, interviewing techniques, and locating job leads.

Individuals not working with a school career services office can check the classified ads for job openings. They also can work with a local employment agency that places computer professionals in appropriate jobs. Many openings in the computer industry are publicized by word of mouth, so you should stay in touch with working computer professionals to learn who is hiring. In addition, these people may be willing to refer you directly to the person in charge of recruiting.

Computer engineers who are interested in working for private aviation and aerospace companies should contact these companies directly for information on employment opportunities. Job seekers who wish to work for NASA should visit http://www.nasajobs.nasa. gov for more information.

ADVANCEMENT

Computer engineers who demonstrate leadership qualities and thorough technical know-how may become *project team leaders* responsible for full-scale software and hardware development projects. Project team leaders oversee the work of technicians and engineers. They determine the overall parameters of a project, calculate time schedules and financial budgets, divide the project into smaller tasks, and assign these tasks to engineers. Overall, they do both managerial and technical work.

Computer engineers with experience as project team leaders may be promoted to a position as *computer manager,* running a large research and development department. Managers oversee software projects with a more encompassing perspective; they help choose projects to be undertaken, select project team leaders and engineering teams, and assign individual projects. In some cases, they may be required to travel, solicit new business, and contribute to the general marketing strategy of the company.

Many computer professionals find that their interests change over time. As long as individuals are well qualified and keep up to date with the latest technology, they are usually able to find positions in other areas of the computer industry.

EARNINGS

Starting salary offers in 2005 for bachelor's degree candidates in computer engineering averaged $52,464, according to the National Association of Colleges and Employers. Candidates with master's degrees averaged $60,354. Engineers employed by NASA earned starting salaries that ranged from $33,151 to $44,034 in 2006.

Software engineers specializing in systems software earned median salaries of $82,120 in 2005. The lowest-paid 10 percent averaged $51,890 annually, and the highest-paid engineers made more than $120,410 per year. Software engineers specializing in applications earned median annual salaries of $77,090 in 2005, according to the U.S. Department of Labor. The lowest 10 percent averaged less than $47,370, and the highest 10 percent earned $116,150 or more annually.

The U.S. Department of Labor reports that median annual earnings of computer hardware engineers were $84,420 in 2005. Salaries ranged from less than $52,470 to more than $128,300.

When computer engineers are promoted to project team leader or computer manager, they can earn even more. Computer engineers generally earn more in geographical areas where there are clusters of computer companies, such as the Silicon Valley in northern California.

Most computer engineers work for companies that offer extensive benefits, including health insurance, sick leave, and paid vacation. In some smaller computer companies, however, benefits may be limited.

WORK ENVIRONMENT

Computer engineers usually work in comfortable office environments. Overall, they usually work 40-hour weeks, but this depends on the nature of the employer and expertise of the engineer. In consulting firms, for example, it is typical for engineers to work long hours and frequently travel to out-of-town assignments.

Computer engineers generally receive an assignment and a time frame within which to accomplish it; daily work details are often left up to the individuals. Some engineers work relatively lightly at the beginning of a project, but work a lot of overtime at the end in order to catch up. Most engineers are not compensated for overtime. Computer engineering can be stressful, especially when engineers must work to meet deadlines. Working with programming languages and intense details, for example, is often frustrating. Therefore, computer engineers should be patient, enjoy problem-solving challenges, and work well under pressure.

OUTLOOK

Employment for software engineers in aerospace product and parts manufacturing will grow by more than 29 percent through 2014, according to the U.S. Department of Labor. Overall, the field of software engineering is expected to be one of the fastest-growing occupations through 2014. Demands made on computers increase every day and from all industries. Rapid growth in the computer systems design and related industries will account for much of this growth. In addition, businesses will continue to implement new and innovative technology to remain competitive, and they will need software engineers to do this. Software engineers will also be needed to handle ever-growing capabilities of computer networks, e-commerce, and wireless technologies, as well as the security features needed to protect such systems from outside attacks.

Employment in hardware engineering will grow about as fast as the average through 2014, according to the U.S. Department of Labor. Foreign competition and increased productivity at U.S. companies will limit opportunities for hardware engineers. Despite this prediction, opportunities are still expected to be good as the number of new graduates entering the field will match the number of engineers leaving the field.

FOR MORE INFORMATION

Contact the AIA for publications with information on aerospace technologies, careers, and space.
   Aerospace Industries Association (AIA)
   1000 Wilson Boulevard, Suite 1700
   Arlington, VA 22209-3928
   Tel: 703-358-1000
   http://www.aia-aerospace.org

For career information and information on student branches of this organization, contact the AIAA.
   American Institute of Aeronautics and Astronautics (AIAA)
   1801 Alexander Bell Drive, Suite 500
   Reston, VA 20191-4344
   Tel: 800-639-2422
   http://www.aiaa.org

For information on internships, student membership, and the student magazine Crossroads, *contact*
   Association for Computing Machinery
   1515 Broadway
   New York, NY 10036-8901
   Tel: 800-342-6626
   http://www.acm.org

For certification information, contact
   Institute for Certification of Computing Professionals
   2350 East Devon Avenue, Suite 115
   Des Plaines, IL 60018-4610
   Tel: 800-843-8227
   Email: office@iccp.org
   http://www.iccp.org

For information on scholarships, student membership, and the student newsletter, looking.forward, *contact*
   IEEE Computer Society
   1730 Massachusetts Avenue, NW

Washington, DC 20036-1992
Tel: 202-371-0101
Email: membership@computer.org
http://www.computer.org

For information on aeronautical careers, internships, and student projects, visit NASA's Web site.
National Aeronautics and Space Administration (NASA)
Public Communications and Inquiries Management Office,
  Suite 1M32
Washington, DC 20546-0001
Tel: 202-358-0001
Email: public-inquiries@hq.nasa.gov
http://www.nasa.gov

INTERVIEW

Lisa Velte is the director of human resources at Analytical Graphics Inc., the leading provider of off the shelf software analysis tools for the space and intelligence industries. She has been employed in the field for more than 20 years. Lisa discussed her career with the editors of Careers in Focus: Space Exploration.

Q. Tell us about Analytical Graphics Inc. (AGI) and the products it creates for the space and intelligence industries.
A. AGI provides software to more than 30,000 national security and space professionals for integrated analyses of land, sea, air, and space assets. Key applications include battlespace management, geospatial intelligence initiatives, space operations, and national defense programs.

Q. What types of workers are employed at AGI?
A. Engineering workers, primarily from the aerospace field, who have achieved all levels of advanced educational attainment—from the bachelor of science through the Ph.D.

Q. What are your primary responsibilities at AGI?
A. My responsibilities at AGI involve the attraction, retention, alignment, and development of top talent as we accomplish our strategic and tactical objectives. This includes recruiting, compensation, benefits, incentives, training, and development. I have had the privilege of recruiting top talent to our organization for 10+ years as well as watching these folks grow and develop in their careers.

Q. **What are the most important personal and professional qualities for people who work at AGI?**

A. Energy, passion, enthusiasm, a customer service mentality (commitment to customer success), a good attitude, aptitude, and alignment with required job tasks.

Q. **What advice would you offer students as they graduate and look for jobs in the space and intelligence industries?**

A. Do what you love. Get involved in as many work-related activities as you can. Be willing to go that extra mile, be positive and enthusiastic about your job, don't be afraid to take the driver's seat in regard to your career, and work with the highest of ethical standards. Don't be afraid to pursue career opportunities at smaller companies, because you will truly develop a breadth of knowledge and get involved in much more of the process.

Q. **What is the future employment outlook in aerospace and related fields?**

A. The future is bright as space-based technology and research is becoming more prevalent.

Industrial Engineers

OVERVIEW

Industrial engineers use their knowledge of various disciplines—including systems engineering, management science, operations research, and fields such as ergonomics—to determine the most efficient and cost-effective methods for industrial production. They are responsible for designing systems that integrate materials, equipment, information, and people in the overall production process. Approximately 13,000 industrial engineers are employed in aerospace product and parts manufacturing in the United States.

HISTORY

In today's industries, manufacturers increasingly depend on industrial engineers to determine the most efficient production techniques and processes. The roots of industrial engineering, however, can be traced to ancient Greece, where records indicate that manufacturing labor was divided among people having specialized skills.

The most significant milestones in industrial engineering, before the field even had an official name, occurred in the 18th century, when a number of inventions were introduced in the textile industry. The first was the flying shuttle that opened the door to the highly automatic weaving we now take for granted. This shuttle allowed one person, rather than two, to weave fabrics wider than ever before. Other innovative devices, such as the power loom and the spinning jenny that increased weaving speed and improved quality, soon followed. By the late 18th century, the Industrial Revolution was in full swing. Innovations in manufacturing were made, standardization

QUICK FACTS

School Subjects
Computer science
Mathematics

Personal Skills
Leadership/management
Technical/scientific

Work Environment
Primarily indoors
Primarily one location

Minimum Education Level
Bachelor's degree

Salary Range
$33,151 to $68,080 to $97,000+

Certification or Licensing
Required by certain states

Outlook
Faster than the average

DOT
012

GOE
05.01.06

NOC
2141

O*NET-SOC
17-2112.00

of interchangeable parts was implemented, and specialization of labor was increasingly put into practice.

Industrial engineering as a science is said to have originated with the work of Frederick Taylor. In 1881, he began to study the way production workers used their time. At the Midvale Steel Company, where he was employed, he introduced the concept of time study, whereby workers were timed with a stopwatch and their production was evaluated. He used the studies to design methods and equipment that allowed tasks to be done more efficiently.

In the early 1900s, the field was known as scientific management. Frank and Lillian Gilbreth were influential with their motion studies of workers performing various tasks. Then, around 1913, automaker Henry Ford implemented a conveyor belt assembly line in his factory, which led to increasingly integrated production lines in more and more companies. Industrial engineers nowadays are called upon to solve ever more complex operating problems and to design systems involving large numbers of workers, complicated equipment, and vast amounts of information. They meet this challenge by utilizing advanced computers and software to design complex mathematical models and other simulations.

THE JOB

Industrial engineers are involved with the development and implementation of the systems and procedures that are utilized by many industries and businesses. In general, they figure out the most effective ways to use the three primary elements of any company: people, facilities, and equipment.

Industrial engineers are key workers in the aviation and aerospace industries. An industrial engineer employed by the National Aeronautics and Space Administration (NASA), for example, might work with an interdisciplinary team of engineers and scientists to ensure that the manufacturing process for a new space vehicle is efficient, as well as safe. Other responsibilities might include devising a method to reduce noise exposure for workers building a new satellite, creating a barcode system that organizes thousands of parts during the production process of a new space exploration vehicle, designing and managing factory layout projects, or comparing production methods at NASA facilities in order to eliminate unnecessary expenditures.

Although industrial engineers work in a variety of businesses, the main focus of the discipline is in manufacturing, also called industrial production. Primarily, industrial engineers are concerned with process technology, which includes the design and layout of machinery and the organization of workers who implement the required tasks.

Industrial engineers have many responsibilities. With regard to facilities and equipment, engineers are involved in selecting machinery and other equipment and then in setting them up in the most efficient production layout. They also develop methods to accomplish production tasks such as the organization of an assembly line. In addition, they devise systems for quality control, distribution, and inventory.

Industrial engineers are responsible for some organizational issues. For instance, they might study an organization chart and other information about a project and then determine the functions and responsibilities of workers. They devise and implement job evaluation procedures as well as articulate labor-utilization standards for workers. Engineers often meet with managers to discuss cost analysis, financial planning, job evaluation, and salary administration. Not only do they recommend methods for improving employee efficiency, but they may also devise wage and incentive programs.

Industrial engineers evaluate ergonomic issues, the relationship between human capabilities and the physical environment in which they work. For example, they might evaluate whether machines are causing physical harm or discomfort to workers or whether the machines could be designed differently to enable workers to be more productive.

REQUIREMENTS

High School

To prepare for a college engineering program, concentrate on mathematics (algebra, trigonometry, geometry, calculus), physical sciences (physics, chemistry), social sciences (economics, sociology), and English. Engineers often have to convey ideas graphically and may need to visualize processes in three-dimension, so courses in graphics, drafting, and design are also helpful. In addition, round out your education with computer science, history, and foreign language classes. If honors-level courses are available to you, be sure to take them.

Postsecondary Training

A bachelor's degree from an accredited institution is usually the minimum requirement for all professional positions. The Accreditation Board for Engineering and Technology (ABET) accredits schools offering engineering programs, including industrial engineering. A listing of accredited colleges and universities is available on the ABET's Web site (http://www.abet.org), and a visit here should be one of your first stops when you are deciding on a school to attend. Colleges and universities offer either four- or five-year engineering programs. Because of the intensity of the curricula, many students take heavy course loads and attend summer sessions in order to finish in four years.

During your junior and senior years of college, you should consider your specific career goals, such as in which industry to work. Third- and fourth-year courses focus on such subjects such as facility planning and design, work measurement standards, process design, engineering economics, manufacturing and automation, and incentive plans.

Many industrial engineers go on to earn graduate degrees. These programs tend to involve more research and independent study. Graduate degrees are usually required for teaching positions.

Certification or Licensing

Licensure as a professional engineer is recommended since an increasing number of employers require it. Even employers who do not require licensing will view it favorably when considering new hires or when reviewing workers for promotion. Licensing requirements vary from state to state. In general, however, they involve having graduated from an accredited school, having four years of work experience, and having passed the eight-hour Fundamentals of Engineering exam and the eight-hour Principles and Practice of Engineering exam. Depending on your state, you can take the Fundamentals exam shortly before your graduation from college or after you have received your bachelor's degree. At that point, you will be an engineer-in-training (EIT). Once you have fulfilled all the licensure requirements, you receive the designation professional engineer (PE).

Other Requirements

Industrial engineers enjoy problem solving and analyzing things as well as being a team member. The ability to communicate is vital since engineers interact with all levels of management and workers. Being organized and detail-minded is important because industrial engineers often handle large projects and must bring them in on time and on budget. Since process design is the cornerstone of the field, an engineer should be creative and inventive.

EXPLORING

Try joining a science or engineering club, such as the Junior Engineering Technical Society (JETS). JETS offers academic competitions in subjects such as computer fundamentals, mathematics, physics, and English. It also conducts design contests in which students learn and apply science and engineering principles. JETS also offers the *Pre-Engineering Times*, a publication that will be useful if you are interested in engineering. It contains information on engineering specialties, competitions, schools, scholarships, and other resources. Visit http://www.jets.org/publications/petimes.cfm to read the publication. You also might read some engineering books for background on the field or magazines such as *Industrial Engineer,* a magazine published by the Institute of Industrial Engineers (IIE). Selected articles from *Industrial Engineer* can be viewed on the IIE's Web site, http://www.iienet.org.

EMPLOYERS

Approximately 13,000 industrial engineers are employed in aerospace product and parts manufacturing in the United States. Although a majority of industrial engineers are employed in the manufacturing industry, related jobs are found in almost all businesses, including aviation; aerospace; transportation; communications; electric; gas and sanitary services; government; finance; insurance; real estate; wholesale and retail trade; construction; mining; agriculture; forestry; and fishing. Also, many work as independent consultants.

STARTING OUT

The main qualification for an entry-level job is a bachelor's degree in industrial engineering. Accredited college programs generally have job openings listed in their career services offices. Entry-level industrial engineers find jobs in various departments, such as computer operations, warehousing, and quality control. As engineers gain on-the-job experience and familiarity with departments, they may decide on a specialty. Some may want to continue to work as process designers or methods engineers, while others may move on to administrative positions. Job seekers who wish to work for NASA should visit http://www.nasajobs.nasa.gov for more information.

Some further examples of specialties include work-measurement standards; shipping and receiving; cost control; engineering economics; materials handling; management information systems;

mathematical models; and operations. Many who choose industrial engineering as a career find its appeal in the diversity of sectors to be explored.

ADVANCEMENT

After having worked at least three years in the same job, an industrial engineer may have the credentials needed for advancement to a higher position. In general, positions in operations and administration are considered high-level jobs, although this varies from company to company. Engineers who work in these areas tend to earn larger salaries than those who work in warehousing or cost control, for example. If one is interested in moving to a different company, it is considered easier to do so within the same industry.

Industrial engineering jobs are often considered stepping-stones to management positions, even in other fields. Engineers with many years' experience frequently are promoted to higher level jobs with greater responsibilities. Because of the field's broad exposure, industrial engineering employees are generally considered better prepared for executive roles than are other types of engineers.

EARNINGS

According to the U.S. Department of Labor, the mean annual wage for industrial engineers employed in aerospace product and parts manufacturing in 2005 was $68,080. The lowest-paid 10 percent of all industrial engineers earned less than $43,620 annually. However, as with most occupations, salaries rise as more experience is gained. Very experienced engineers can earn more than $97,000. According to a survey by the National Association of Colleges and Employers, the average starting salary for industrial engineers with a bachelor's degree was $49,567 in 2005, while those with a master's degree earned $56,561 a year; and with a Ph.D., $85,000. Engineers employed by NASA earned starting salaries that ranged from $33,151 to $44,034 in 2006.

WORK ENVIRONMENT

Industrial engineers usually work in offices at desks and computers, designing and evaluating plans, statistics, and other documents. Overall, industrial engineering is ranked above other engineering disciplines for factors such as employment outlook, salary, and physical environment. However, industrial engineering jobs are considered stressful because they often entail tight deadlines and demanding quotas, and jobs are moderately competitive. Engineers work an average of 46 hours per week.

Industrial engineers generally collaborate with other employees, conferring on designs and procedures, as well as with business managers and consultants. Although they spend most of their time in their offices, they frequently must evaluate conditions at factories and plants, where noise levels are often high.

OUTLOOK

The U.S. Department of Labor anticipates that employment for industrial engineers employed in aerospace product and parts manufacturing will grow faster than the average for all occupations through 2014. The demand for industrial engineers will continue as aerospace companies strive to make their production processes more effective and competitive. Engineers who transfer or retire will create the highest percentage of openings in this field.

FOR MORE INFORMATION

For a list of ABET-accredited engineering schools, contact
Accreditation Board for Engineering and Technology (ABET)
111 Market Place, Suite 1050
Baltimore, MD 21202-7116
Tel: 410-347-7700
http://www.abet.org

Contact the AIA for publications with information on aerospace technologies, careers, and space.
Aerospace Industries Association (AIA)
1000 Wilson Boulevard, Suite 1700
Arlington, VA 22209-3928
Tel: 703-358-1000
http://www.aia-aerospace.org

For career information and information on student branches of this organization, contact the AIAA.
American Institute of Aeronautics and Astronautics (AIAA)
1801 Alexander Bell Drive, Suite 500
Reston, VA 20191-4344
Tel: 800-639-2422
http://www.aiaa.org

For comprehensive information about careers in industrial engineering, contact

Institute of Industrial Engineers
3577 Parkway Lane, Suite 200
Norcross, GA 30092-2833
Tel: 800-494-0460
http://www.iienet.org

Visit the JETS Web site for membership information and to read the online brochure Industrial Engineering.

Junior Engineering Technical Society (JETS)
1420 King Street, Suite 405
Alexandria, VA 22314-2750
Tel: 703-548-5387
Email: info@jets.org
http://www.jets.org

For information on aeronautical careers, internships, and student projects, visit NASA's Web site.

National Aeronautics and Space Administration (NASA)
Public Communications and Inquiries Management Office
Suite 1M32
Washington, DC 20546-0001
Tel: 202-358-0001
Email: public-inquiries@hq.nasa.gov
http://www.nasa.gov

Materials Engineers

OVERVIEW

Materials engineers extract, process, create, design, and test materials—such as metals, ceramics, plastics, semiconductors, and combinations of these materials called composites—to create a wide variety of products. Approximately 1,800 materials engineers are employed in the aerospace product and parts manufacturing industry.

HISTORY

Physical metallurgy as a modern science dates back to 1890, when a group of metallurgists began the study of alloys. Enormous advances were made in the 20th century, including the development of stainless steel, the discovery of a strong but lightweight aluminum, and the increased use of magnesium and its alloys.

Not until the scientific and industrial revolutions of the 19th century did people begin to use ceramics in complex scientific and industrial processes. Individuals skilled with ceramic materials began to develop new, manmade materials to be used in high-technology applications. New uses were also developed for naturally occurring materials, which made possible the development of new products that were stronger, more transparent, or more magnetic. The earliest ceramic engineers used porcelains for high-voltage electrical insulation. Ceramic engineers benefited other industries as well, developing, for example, material for spark plugs (automotive and aerospace industries) and magnetic and semiconductor materials (electronics industry). Today, basic ceramic materials such as clay and sand are being used not only

QUICK FACTS

School Subjects
Computer science
Mathematics
Physics

Personal Skills
Mechanical/manipulative
Technical/scientific

Work Environment
Primarily indoors
Primarily one location

Minimum Education Level
Bachelor's degree

Salary Range
$33,151 to $78,150 to $105,330+

Certification or Licensing
Required for certain positions

Outlook
About as fast as the average

DOT
006, 011, 019

GOE
02.01.02, 05.01.07

NOC
2134, 2142

O*NET-SOC
17-2131.00, 19-2032.00

by artists and craftspeople but also by engineers to create a variety of products—memory storage, optical communications, and electronics.

It was not until 1909 that the Belgian-American chemist Leo H. Baekeland produced the first synthetic plastic. This product replaced natural rubber in electrical insulation and was used for phone handsets and automobile distributor caps and rotors, and is still used today. Other plastics materials were developed steadily. Today, plastics manufacturing is a major industry whose products play a vital role in many other industries and activities around the world. It is difficult to find an area of our lives where plastic does not play some role.

Today, the fields of metallurgical, ceramics, and plastics engineering have become so closely linked that they are now often referred to as materials engineering to reflect their interdisciplinary nature.

Materials engineers played a key role in the accident investigation of the Space Shuttle *Columbia,* which was destroyed during reentry into the Earth's atmosphere in 2003. The accident was caused by foam that broke off and damaged the shuttle's reinforced carbon-carbon panels and thermal protection tiles—allowing superheated gases to enter the shuttle during reentry. Engineers studied the foam, panels, and tiles and made recommendations to help the National Aeronautics and Space Administration (NASA) avoid future accidents.

THE JOB

Materials engineers employed in the aviation and aerospace industries determine the suitability of the various materials that are used to produce aerospace vehicles and other types of equipment and machinery used for space exploration. For example, materials engineers employed by NASA might be assigned to help develop a new heat shield for the Crew Exploration Vehicle, which will replace the space shuttle in 2011. Others might develop new aluminum-silicon alloys that can be used in engines for spacecrafts. These alloys are lighter and more durable—improving engine performance and durability. Finally, other materials engineers might conduct long-term studies on the effects of space (extreme temperatures, radiation, corrosive atomic oxygen, meteorites, and the absence of atmosphere and gravity) on materials used in the construction of spacecraft and other components.

Several types of engineering subspecialties exist under the umbrella term "materials engineer." These include *metallurgical engineers; ceramic engineers;* and *polymer,* or *plastics, engineers.*

Metallurgical Engineers

Metals are at the core of every manufacturing society. Parts made from metal are incorporated in a wide variety of products, from steel and iron used in building materials and automobile parts, to aluminum used in packaging, to titanium used in aerospace and military aircraft applications such as bulkheads, fasteners, and landing gear. Metallurgy is the art and science of extracting metals from ores found in nature and preparing them for use by alloying, shaping, and heating them.

Metallurgical engineers are specialists who develop extraction and manufacturing processes for the metals industry. Metallurgical engineers develop new types of metal alloys and adapt existing materials to new uses. They manipulate the atomic and molecular structure of materials in controlled manufacturing environments, selecting materials with desirable mechanical, electrical, magnetic, chemical, and heat-transfer properties that meet specific performance requirements. Metallurgical engineers are sometimes also referred to as *metallurgists.*

Ceramic Engineers

Today, basic ceramic materials such as clay and sand are being used by engineers to create a variety of products—the ceramic tiles that shield the space shuttle from excessive heat during reentry (where temperatures reach 3000° F) into the Earth's atmosphere, memory storage, optical communications, and electronics. Ceramic engineers are working with more advanced materials as well (many produced by chemical processes), including high-strength silicon carbides, nitrides, and fracture-resistant zirconias. Like other materials engineers, ceramic engineers work toward the development of new products. They also use their scientific knowledge to anticipate new applications for existing products.

Plastics Engineers

Today, synthetic polymers—chains of hydrocarbon molecules—represent a multi-million dollar business as either the main ingredient or the item itself in aerospace, building and construction, clothing, packaging, and consumer products. In addition, plastics has had a stunning effect on the automotive, biomedical, communications, electrical and electronic fields, in some cases breathing new life into them.

Plastics engineers perform a wide variety of duties depending on the type of company they work for and the products it produces. Plastics engineers, for example, might design and manufacture lightweight parts for aircraft and automobiles, or create new plastics to replace metallic or wood parts that have come to be too expensive or hard to obtain. Others may be employed to formulate less-expensive, fire-resistant plastics for use in the construction of houses, offices, and factories. Plastics engineers may also develop new types of bio-degradable molecules that are friendly to the environment, reducing pollution and increasing recyclability.

Plastics engineers perform a variety of duties. Some of their specific job titles and duties include: *plastics application engineers,* who develop new processes and materials in order to create a better finished product; *plastics process engineers,* who oversee the production of reliable, high quality, standard materials; and *plastics research specialists,* who use the basic building blocks of matter to discover and create new materials.

REQUIREMENTS

High School

While few courses at the high school level are directly related to materials engineering, the foundation for engineering includes a wide range of math and science courses. If you are interested in pursuing a career in this field you should invest in an education steeped heavily in math and science, including geometry, algebra, trigonometry, calculus, chemistry, biology, physics, and computer programming. Materials engineers who will also be designing products will need drafting skills, so mechanical drawing and art classes are an excellent choice.

English, speech, and foreign language classes will help you develop strong communication skills and provide you with the opportunity to learn how to better express yourself.

Ancillary interests should not be overlooked. In addition to providing you with possible ways of applying your scientific knowledge in enjoyable, recreational activities, exploring personal hobbies can also develop crucial personal and professional qualities and skills, such as patience, perseverance, and creative problem-solving.

Postsecondary Training

If your career goal is to become a materials engineer, you will need a bachelor of science degree in materials, metallurgical engineering, ceramic engineering, plastics engineering, or a related field. Degrees are granted in many different specializations by more than 80 universities and colleges in the United States.

There are a wide variety of programs available at colleges and universities, and it is helpful to explore as many of these programs as possible, especially those that are accredited by the Accreditation Board for Engineering and Technology (http://www.abet.org). Some programs prepare students for practical design and production work; others concentrate on theoretical science and mathematics. More than 50 percent of materials engineers begin their first job with a bachelor's degree.

Many engineers continue on for a master's degree either immediately after graduation or after a few years of work experience. A master's degree generally takes two years of study. A doctoral degree requires at least four years of study and research beyond the bachelor's degree and is usually completed by engineers interested in research or teaching at the college level.

Certification or Licensing

Licensing is not generally required for most materials engineering professions. However, licensing is recommended to enhance your credentials and make yourself open to more job opportunities.

In general, the licensing process for all branches of engineering results in the formal designation of Professional Engineer (PE). Requirements vary from state to state but generally it takes about four to five years to become a licensed PE. Many engineers begin the process while still in college by taking the Fundamentals of Engineering (FE) exam, an eight-hour test that covers everything from electronics, chemistry, mathematics, and physics to the more advanced engineering issues.

Once a candidate has successfully passed the FE exam, the next requirement to fulfill is to acquire four years of progressive engineering experience. Some states require that materials engineers obtain experience under the supervision of a PE. Once a candidate has four years of on-the-job experience, he or she then takes another exam specific to their engineering area (each branch of engineering has its own specialized, upper-level test). Candidates who successfully complete this examination are officially referred to as Professional Engineers. Without this designation, engineers aren't allowed to refer to themselves as PEs or function in the same legal capacity as PEs.

Other Requirements

With new products being developed daily, materials engineers are constantly under pressure to integrate new technology and science. Having the imagination to consider all of the possibilities and then being versatile enough to adapt one application of a metal, ceramic, polymer, or other material to another situation are perhaps the most essential qualities for materials engineers. To accomplish this, materials engineers must first learn how the material may be applicable to their industry or product line and then decide how to adjust their current manufacturing process to incorporate it.

In addition to having a good mechanical aptitude for developing parts and tooling, one of the more basic qualities for any student considering a career in materials engineering is a solid understanding of the properties of the material they work with it—be it metals, ceramics, polymers, or a composite of these materials.

As in every scientific endeavor, there are always a varying number of factors which influence the outcome of the experiment, and the chemical configurations of a specific material is no different. It takes an individual with an extraordinary amount of patience, focus, and determination to notice precisely what factors are achieving the desired results. Successful materials engineers pay attention to the smallest detail, note the nuances between experiments, and then use that information to develop further tests or theories. Having a certain amount of critical distance helps materials engineers step back from the minutia and reassess the direction in which they're headed.

Materials engineers need to be inquisitive, to take creative steps toward improvements by constantly asking questions and to take a fresh look at familiar practices.

Good communication skills are vital for success in engineering. You may be required to write reports and present your research before large audiences at industry seminars.

EXPLORING

If you're interested in materials engineering, it's a good idea to take on special research assignments from teachers who can provide guidance on topics and methods. There are also summer academic programs where students with similar interests can spend a week or more in a special environment. It's also a good idea to join a national science club, such as the Junior Engineering Technical Society. In this organization, member students have the opportunity to compete in academic events, take career exploration tests, and enter design contests where they build models of such things as spacecraft and other structures based on their own designs.

For hands-on experience with materials, take pottery, sculpture, or metalworking classes; this will allow you to become familiar with materials such as clay, glass, and metals.

EMPLOYERS

Upon graduation most materials engineers go to work in industry. In industry, materials engineers fall into five main employment groups: manufacturing (where the products are made and tested); material applications and development; machinery/equipment (which requires advanced knowledge of mechanical engineering); government positions; and consulting (where you will need your Professional Engineer licensing). Approximately 1,800 materials engineers are employed in the aerospace product and parts manufacturing industry. Others specialize in computer and electronic products, fabricated metal products, transportation equipment, machinery manufacturing, and primary metal production.

Some materials engineers may continue their studies and go on to teach in higher education. Most materials programs have advanced programs for master's and doctoral studies.

STARTING OUT

As a high school senior, you might want to inquire with established aviation, aerospace, and other manufacturing companies about internships and summer employment opportunities. College career services offices can also help you find employers that participate in cooperative education programs, where high school students work at materials engineering jobs in exchange for course credits.

Most materials engineers find their first job through their colleges' career services office. Technical recruiters visit universities and colleges annually to interview graduating students and possibly offer them jobs. Materials engineers can also find work by directly applying to companies, through job listings at state and private employment services or in classified advertisements in newspapers and trade publications. Job seekers who wish to work for NASA should visit http://www.nasajobs.nasa.gov for more information.

ADVANCEMENT

In general, advancing through the ranks of materials engineers is similar to advancement in other disciplines. Working in entry-level positions usually means executing the research, plans, or theories which someone else has originated. With additional experience and education, materials engineers begin to tackle projects solo or, at least, accept responsibility for organizing and managing them for a supervisor. Those materials engineers with advanced degrees (or, at this point in time, a great deal of experience) can move into supervisory or administrative positions within any one of the major categories, such as research, development, or design. Eventually, materials engineers who have distinguished themselves by consistently producing successful projects, and who have polished their business and managerial skills, will advance to become the directors of engineering for an entire plant or research division.

EARNINGS

Materials engineers are among the highest-paid engineers in the engineering professions. The U.S. Department of Labor reports that materials engineers employed in aerospace product and parts manufacturing earned mean salaries of $78,150 in 2005. At the low end of the scale, 10 percent of all materials engineers earned less than $44,090 annually in 2005. The highest-paid 10 percent had annual incomes of more than $105,330 during this same time period. Starting salaries for those with bachelor's degrees in materials engineering averaged approximately $50,982 in 2005, according to a survey by the National Association of Colleges and Employers. Engineers employed by NASA earned starting salaries that ranged from $33,151 to $44,034 in 2006. Salaries for government workers are generally less than those who work for private companies.

Materials engineers can expect a good benefits package, including paid sick, holiday, vacation, and personal time; medical coverage; stock options; 401 (k) plans; and other perks, depending on the company and industry.

WORK ENVIRONMENT

Working conditions in materials engineering positions vary depending on the specific field and department in which one works. Hands-on engineers work in plants and factories. Researchers work mainly in laboratories, research institutes, and universities. Those in management positions work mostly in offices; and teachers, of course, work in school environments. Whatever the job description, a materials engineer typically works a standard eight-hour day, five days a week. These engineers work in an office, a research lab, a classroom, or a manufacturing plant.

OUTLOOK

Employment in the aerospace product and parts manufacturing industry is expected to grow more slowly than the average through 2014, according to the U.S. Department of Labor. Despite this prediction, materials engineers should continue to have good job prospects due to their key role in designing and testing materials used in space exploration. The field of materials engineering is small, and the number of students pursuing study in this discipline is low. This should create opportunities for aspiring materials engineers. Materials engineers will also be needed, of course, to replace those who leave the field for retirement or other work. The U.S. Department of Labor predicts that materials engineers who specialize in nanomaterials (those at the near-atomic level) and biomaterials (natural or synthetic materials used to manufacture prostheses, implants, and surgical instruments) will have especially strong employment prospects.

FOR MORE INFORMATION

Contact the AIA for publications with information on aerospace technologies, careers, and space.
Aerospace Industries Association (AIA)
1000 Wilson Boulevard, Suite 1700
Arlington, VA 22209-3928
Tel: 703-358-1000
http://www.aia-aerospace.org

Contact the society for an overview of ceramics, information on student chapters, a list of colleges and universities that offer materials engineering programs, and a list of how ceramics have played a role in the top achievements in engineering.
American Ceramic Society
735 Ceramic Place, Suite 100
Westerville, OH 43081-8728
Tel: 614-890-4700
Email: info@ceramics.org
http://www.ceramics.org

For career information and information on student branches of this organization, contact the AIAA.
American Institute of Aeronautics and Astronautics (AIAA)
1801 Alexander Bell Drive, Suite 500
Reston, VA 20191-4344
Tel: 800-639-2422
http://www.aiaa.org

Contact this organization for information on materials engineering careers, scholarships, educational programs, and job listings.
ASM International
9639 Kinsman Road
Materials Park, OH 44073-0002
Tel: 800-336-5152
Email: CustomerService@asminternational.org
http://www.asm-intl.org

JETS has career information and offers high school students the opportunity to "try on" engineering through a number of programs and competitions. For more information, contact
Junior Engineering Technical Society Inc. (JETS)
1420 King Street, Suite 405
Alexandria, VA 22314-2794
Tel: 703-548-5387
Email: info@jets.org
http://www.jets.org

The society offers information on ceramics, materials, and metallurgical engineering programs, careers, scholarships, and student chapters.
The Minerals, Metals & Materials Society
184 Thorn Hill Road
Warrendale, PA 15086-7514
Tel: 800-759-4867
Email: tmsgeneral@tms.org
http://www.tms.org

For information on aeronautical careers, internships, and student projects, visit NASA's Web site.
National Aeronautics and Space Administration (NASA)
Public Communications and Inquiries Management Office,
Suite 1M32
Washington, DC 20546-0001
Tel: 202-358-0001
Email: public-inquiries@hq.nasa.gov
http://www.nasa.gov

This organization offers information on mining engineering, education, accredited schools, and student membership.
Society for Mining, Metallurgy, and Exploration
8307 Shaffer Parkway

Littleton, CO 80127-4102
Tel: 800-763-3132
Email: sme@smenet.org
http://www.smenet.org

Contact the SPE for information on careers in plastics engineering and scholarships.
Society of Plastics Engineers (SPE)
14 Fairfield Drive
Brookfield, CT 06804-0403
Tel: 203-775-0471
Email: info@4spe.org
http://www.4spe.org

Mathematicians

OVERVIEW

A *mathematician* solves or directs the solution of problems in higher mathematics, including algebra, geometry, number theory, logic, and topology. *Theoretical mathematicians* work with the relationships among mathematical forms and the underlying principles that can be applied to problems, including electronic data processing and military planning. *Applied mathematicians* develop the techniques and approaches to problem solving in the physical, biological, and social sciences. Approximately 2,500 mathematicians are employed in nonacademic settings in the United States.

HISTORY

Although mathematics may be considered a "pure" science—that is, one that may be studied for its own sake—math has often been applied to produce engineering and other scientific achievements. The non-Euclidean geometry developed by Bernard Riemann in 1854 seemed quite impractical at the time, yet some years later Albert Einstein used it as part of his work in the development of his theory of relativity. Einstein's theory similarly appeared to have no practical application at the time but later became the basis for work in nuclear energy.

Mathematics is a discipline used in the study of all sciences. In addition to contributing to the development of nuclear energy, mathematicians played important roles in the 20th century in the development of the automobile, the television, and space exploration. They have been instrumental in advancing research and experimental efforts in sociology, psychology, and education, among other fields. The development of space vehicles and electronic computers are but two examples that characterize the dynamic nature and increasing importance of mathematicians in the 21st century. Mathematicians, although working in one of the oldest and most fundamental of sciences, are always contributing new ideas.

THE JOB

There are two broad areas of opportunity in mathematics: theoretical and applied. In addition, mathematicians may choose to pursue a career in teaching. The duties performed, the processes involved, the work situations encountered, and the equipment used vary considerably, depending on the institutional or organizational setting.

Theoretical mathematicians deal with pure and abstract mathematical concepts rather than the practical application of such concepts to everyday problems. They might teach in a college or university or work in the research department of a business or government office. They are concerned with the advancement of mathematical knowledge, the logical development of mathematical systems, and the study and analysis of relationships among mathematical forms. "Pure" mathematicians focus their efforts mainly on problems dealing with mathematical principles and reasoning.

Applied mathematicians develop and apply mathematical knowledge to practical and research problems in the social, physical, life, and Earth sciences. Business, industry, and government agencies such as the National Aeronautics and Space Administration (NASA) rely heavily on applied mathematicians, particularly for research and development programs. Therefore, it is necessary for these mathematicians to be knowledgeable about their employer's operations and products as well as their own field. Applied mathematicians work on problems ranging from the stability of rockets to the effects of new drugs on disease.

The applied and theoretical aspects of mathematicians' work are not always clearly separated. Some mathematicians, usually those dealing with the application of mathematics, may become involved in both aspects. In addition to having general knowledge about modern computing equipment, mathematicians need some basic experience in computer programming and operation because of the rapidly expanding reliance on computers.

Specialists in the field of applied mathematics include the following:

Computer applications engineers formulate mathematical models and develop computer systems to solve scientific and engineering problems.

Engineering analysts apply logical analysis to scientific, engineering, and other technical problems and convert them to mathematical terms to be solved by digital computers.

Operations research analysts employ mathematics to solve management and operational problems.

Weight analysts are concerned with weight, balance, loading, and operational functions of space vehicles, ships, aircraft, missiles, research instrumentation, and commercial and industrial products and systems. These mathematicians use computers to analyze weight factors and work with design engineers to coordinate their specifications with product development.

Mathematics teachers instruct students at the middle school and high school levels. In high school, they provide instruction in more complex mathematics such as algebra, geometry, trigonometry, pre-calculus, and calculus.

College mathematics professors provide instruction to future mathematicians and students in other disciplines. They often teach courses at various levels of difficulty. Professors usually spend less time in the classroom than high school teachers, but they may have many other responsibilities, including advising doctoral candidates, serving on university or mathematical organization committees, and reading mathematical books and journals. Some professors are also actively involved in research and in contributing to the development of the field; this often includes writing and submitting articles on their research to mathematical journals.

REQUIREMENTS

High School

To pursue a career as a mathematician, take all the math classes that can fit into your schedule. Meet with teachers to get as much insight as you can about doing well in the math courses offered at your school. These courses should include algebra, geometry, trigonometry, and calculus. If your school offers college prep courses, you may be able to study probability, statistics, and logic. Classes such as English composition and computer science are also important.

Postsecondary Training

Undergraduate mathematical study includes work in algebra, geometry, numerical analysis, topology, and statistics. Typical university courses include differential equations, linear algebra, advanced calculus, number theory, and theory and application of digital computers.

In addition to these and other courses from which you may choose as a math major, you should sample broadly in the humanities and the various social, physical, and life sciences.

With the exception of secondary school teaching and working for the federal government, the educational requirement for this profession is a doctoral degree in mathematics. A doctorate is necessary for most research and development positions as well as for college-level teaching. Approximately 200 colleges and universities offer a master's degree, and over 200 offer a Ph.D. in pure or applied mathematics.

Many colleges and universities require that if you major in math you must also take classes in an area related to math, such as computer science, engineering, physical science, or economics.

Certification or Licensing
If you're interested in teaching math in a public elementary school or high school, you must be licensed. However, you usually do not need a license to teach in a private school. Requirements vary from state to state, although all states require that you have at least a bachelor's degree and have finished an approved teacher-training program.

Government positions usually require that applicants take a civil service examination in addition to meeting certain specified requirements that vary according to the type and level of position.

Other Requirements
Being a mathematician requires abilities in abstract reasoning, analyzing, and interpreting mathematical ideas. Speed and accuracy with numbers are necessary skills, too. Finally, communication skills are important because you will often need to interact with others, many of whom may not have an extensive knowledge of mathematics.

EXPLORING

While in high school, you may wish to accelerate your studies by enrolling in summer-session programs offering regular or elective mathematics courses. Some schools have specialized mathematics honors or advanced-placement courses that are part of their regular summer or evening school programs. Ask your math teacher or guidance counselor if there are any mathematics competitions you can enter. Not only can they be fun, but competitions may offer college scholarships as awards.

Interesting Web Sites

AeroSpaceGuide: Space Projects
http://www.aerospaceguide.net

Ask an Astronomer for Kids
http://coolcosmos.ipac.caltech.edu/cosmic_kids/AskKids/index.shtml

Ask the Space Scientist
http://image.gsfc.nasa.gov/poetry/ask/askmag.html

Astrometry.org
http://www.astrometry.org

Astronomy Today
http://www.astronomytoday.com

National Aeronautics and Space Administration
http://www.nasa.gov

NightSkyInfo.com
http://www.nightskyinfo.com

Smithsonian National Air and Space Museum
http://www.nasm.si.edu

SpaceBuffs.com
http://www.spacebuffs.com

SpaceWeather.com
http://www.spaceweather.com

The Woman Astronomer
http://www.womanastronomer.com

Summer and part-time employment with NASA or industrial firms can also provide you with valuable experience and offer the opportunity to test your knowledge, interests, abilities, and personal characteristics in a practical work setting.

EMPLOYERS

Mathematicians hold approximately 2,500 jobs in the federal and state government and in various private industries and business. An additional 53,000 mathematicians work in mathematical faculty positions in colleges and universities.

In government, the Department of Defense and NASA are the main employers of mathematicians. Significant employers in industry include management and public relations; research and testing; aerospace; securities and commodities; and drug manufacturing companies. Other positions are held in such businesses as banks, insurance companies, securities and commodity exchanges, and public utilities.

STARTING OUT

Most college career services offices assist students in finding positions in business and industry upon graduation. Teaching positions in high schools are usually obtained by personal contacts through friends, relatives, or college professors or through college placement offices and by application and interviews. College and university assistantships, instructorships, and professorships often are obtained by departmental recommendations.

Positions in federal, state, and local governments are usually announced well in advance of the required civil service examination, and students can check for such notices on bulletin boards in their college career services offices or other locations such as post offices and government buildings.

ADVANCEMENT

Numerous opportunities for advancement to higher-level positions or into related areas of employment are available to mathematicians. Promotions of mathematicians are generally made on the basis of advanced preparation, knowledge of a specific application, individual appraisal by a superior, or competitive examination.

Opportunities in related fields such as statistics, accounting, actuarial work, and computers allow mathematicians to change their profession, relocate geographically, or advance to better positions with higher salaries.

EARNINGS

Mathematicians' incomes vary with their level of training and the work setting in which they are employed. According to the U.S. Department of Labor, median annual earnings of mathematicians were $80,920 in 2005. Salaries ranged from less than $41,750 to more than $121,770. In 2005, the average yearly salary for mathematicians in government was $88,194. Mathematical statisticians earned an average of $91,446 a year, and *cryptanalysts* (mathematicians who analyze and decipher coding systems to transmit military, political, financial, or law enforcement information) earned $70,774 according to the *Occupational Outlook Handbook*.

Mathematicians receive traditional benefits such as health insurance, vacation time, and sick leave. Teachers usually have more time off during semester breaks and summer vacations, although they are occupied with tasks such as grading papers and advising students.

WORK ENVIRONMENT

The mathematician in industrial and government positions usually works a regular 40-hour week. Those who work in educational settings may have varied schedules. For both, the work environment is generally pleasant and typical of the modern, well-equipped office. The work may require long periods of close concentration. Professional mathematicians who work with or near computers usually work in air-conditioned buildings, as computers are extremely sensitive to temperature changes.

OUTLOOK

Overall employment of mathematicians is expected to decline through 2014. However, it is expected that there will be more jobs in applied mathematics (and related areas such as computer programming, operations research, and engineering design) than in theoretical research. Those who have a background in another field in addition to mathematics (such as computer science and software development, physics, engineering, or operations research) will have more opportunities. The Society for Industrial and Applied Mathematics predicts that opportunities will be good in the following emerging fields: computational biology and genomics, data-mining (including applications in astrophysics), neuroscience, materials science (including applications in aerospace, biology, electronics, and engineering), and computer animation and digital imaging.

Individuals with only a bachelor's degree in mathematics are not qualified for most mathematician jobs. However, those with a double major will have more opportunities. Holders of bachelor's or master's degrees in mathematics who also meet state certification requirements can find jobs as high school mathematics teachers. For mathematicians with a master's degree but no doctorate, jobs may be harder to find. Strong competition will exist for jobs in theoretical research. More openings should be available in applied areas such as computer science and data processing.

FOR MORE INFORMATION

For a variety of useful resources about mathematics, including A Guide to Online Resources for High School Math Students, *visit the AMS's Web site.*

American Mathematical Society (AMS)
201 Charles Street
Providence, RI 02904-2294
Tel: 800-321-4AMS
Email: ams@ams.org
http://www.ams.org

For information on opportunities for women in mathematics, contact
Association for Women in Mathematics
11240 Waples Mill Road, Suite 200
Fairfax, VA 22030-6078
Tel: 703-934-0163
Email: awm@awm-math.org
http://www.awm-math.org

For information on teaching careers in mathematics, contact
National Council of Teachers of Mathematics
1906 Association Drive
Reston, VA 20191-1502
Tel: 703-620-9840
http://www.nctm.org

For information on publications (including Thinking of a Career in Applied Mathematics), *conferences, activity groups, and programs, contact*
Society for Industrial and Applied Mathematics
3600 University City Science Center
Philadelphia, PA 19104-2699
Tel: 215-382-9800
http://www.siam.org

Mechanical Engineers

OVERVIEW

Mechanical engineers plan and design tools, engines, machines, and other mechanical systems that produce, transmit, or use power. They may work in design, instrumentation, testing, robotics, transportation, or bioengineering, among other areas. The broadest of all engineering disciplines, mechanical engineering extends across many interdependent specialties. Mechanical engineers may work in production operations, maintenance, or technical sales, and many are administrators or managers. Mechanical engineers employed in the aerospace industry may work for government agencies such as the National Aeronautics and Space Administration (NASA) or for private corporations such as Boeing, Teledyne Technologies Inc., or Global Aerospace Corporation. There are approximately 13,300 mechanical engineers employed in aerospace product and parts manufacturing in the United States.

HISTORY

The modern field of mechanical engineering took root during the Renaissance. In this period, engineers focused their energies on developing more efficient ways to perform such ordinary tasks as grinding grain and pumping water. Water wheels and windmills were common energy producers at that time. Leonardo da Vinci, who attempted to design such complex machines as a submarine and a helicopter, best personified the burgeoning mechanical inventiveness of the period. One of the Renaissance's most significant inventions was the mechanical clock, powered first by falling weights and later by compressed springs.

Despite these developments, it was not until the Industrial Revolution that mechanical engineering took on its modern form. The steam engine, an efficient power producer, was introduced in 1712 by Thomas Newcomen to pump water from English mines. More than a half century later, James Watt modified Newcomen's engine to power industrial machines. In 1876, a German, Nicolaus Otto, developed the internal combustion engine, which became one of the century's most important inventions. In 1847, a group of British engineers who specialized in steam engines and machine tools organized the Institution of Mechanical Engineers. The American Society of Mechanical Engineers was founded in 1880.

Mechanical engineering rapidly expanded in the 20th century. Mass production systems allowed large quantities of standardized goods to be made at a low cost, and mechanical engineers played a pivotal role in the design of these systems. In the second half of the 20th century, computers revolutionized production. Mechanical engineers now design mechanical systems on computers, and they are used to test, monitor, and analyze mechanical systems and factory production. Mechanical engineers are key players in countless industries, including the aviation and aerospace industries.

THE JOB

The work of a mechanical engineer begins with research and development. A private aerospace company, for example, may need to develop a more fuel-efficient aircraft engine, or engineers employed by NASA may be asked to create a cooling and heating system for the crew exploration vehicle, which will replace the space shuttle. A mechanical engineer working in the research department explores the project's theoretical, mechanical, and material challenges. The engineer may perform experiments to gather necessary data and acquire new knowledge. Often, an experimental device, such as a flight demonstrator, or system is developed. A mechanical engineer may be assigned to oversee the design, development, and testing of the flight demonstrator, which will test and validate various technologies during orbital flight, reentry, and landing of the crew exploration vehicle or other vehicles or technologies.

The *design engineer* takes information gained from research and development and uses it to plan commercially useful products, for example, photonic systems. The aircraft industry uses such systems of lasers for gyroscopic compasses; military uses include systems for avionic platforms, navigation, defense, and search and rescue missions. After the product has been designed and a prototype developed, the product is analyzed by *testing engineers*. Engineers working for the military, for example, could fine tune a "photon pistol" capable of shooting the secret code to launch defense missiles. Design and testing engineers continue to work together until the "photon pistol" could send its particles of light accurately and to some distance along fiber optic cables. Once the final design is set, it is the job of the *manufacturing engineer* to come up with the most time- and cost-efficient way of making the product without sacrificing quality. The amount of factory floor space, the type of manufacturing equipment and machinery, and the cost of labor and materials are some of the factors that must be considered. Engineers select the necessary equipment and machines and oversee their arrangement and safe operation. Mechanical engineers often need to work closely with other specialists such as chemical, avionics, electrical, and industrial engineers to finish the project.

Some types of mechanical systems, such as a telescope used for space and planetary exploration, are so sophisticated that mechanical engineers are needed for operation and ongoing maintenance. For example, numerous mechanical engineers are assigned to monitor, repair, and improve delicate components such as detector mounts and shutter mechanisms on NASA's Hubble Space Telescope. With the help of computers, *maintenance and operations engineers* use their specialized knowledge to monitor complex production systems and make necessary adjustments.

Mechanical engineers also work in marketing, sales, and administration. Because of their training in mechanical engineering, *sales engineers* can give customers a detailed explanation of how a machine or system works. They may also be able to alter its design to meet a customer's needs.

In a small company, a mechanical engineer may need to perform many, if not most, of the above responsibilities. Some tasks might be assigned to *consulting engineers*, who are either self-employed or work for a consulting firm. At large government organizations such as NASA, a mechanical engineer may just focus on one of the above responsibilities.

Other mechanical engineers may work in a number of specialized areas. *Energy specialists* work with power production machines to supply clean and efficient energy for space- and aircraft. *Application engineers* specialize in computer-aided design systems. *Structural analysts* may monitor the static, fatigue, and stress damage to mechanical systems of military aircraft or spacecraft.

REQUIREMENTS

High School

If you are interested in mechanical engineering as a career, you need to take courses in geometry, trigonometry, and calculus. Physics and chemistry courses are also recommended, as is mechanical drawing or computer-aided design, if they are offered at your high school. Communication skills are important for mechanical engineers because they interact with a variety of coworkers and vendors and are often required to prepare and/or present reports. English and speech classes are also helpful. Finally, because computers are such an important part of engineering, computer science courses are good choices.

Postsecondary Training

A bachelor's degree in mechanical engineering is usually the minimum educational requirement for entering this field. A master's degree or even a Ph.D. may be necessary to obtain some positions, such as those in research, teaching, and administration.

In the United States, there are more than 280 colleges and universities where mechanical engineering programs have been approved by the Accreditation Board for Engineering and Technology. Although admissions requirements vary slightly from school to school, most require a solid background in mathematics and science.

In a four-year undergraduate program, students typically begin by studying mathematics and science subjects such as calculus, differential equations, physics, and chemistry. Course work in liberal arts and elementary mechanical engineering is also taken. By the third year, students begin to study the technical core subjects of mechanical engineering—mechanics, thermodynamics, fluid mechanics, design manufacturing, and heat transfer—as well as such specialized topics as power generation and transmission, computer-aided design systems, and the properties of materials.

At some schools, a five- or six-year program combines classroom study with practical experience working for an engineering firm or a government agency such as NASA. Although these cooperative, or work-study, programs take longer, they offer significant advantages. Not only does the salary help pay for educational expenses, but the student has the opportunity to apply theoretical knowledge to actual work problems in mechanical engineering. In some cases, the company or government agency may offer full-time employment to its co-op workers after graduation.

A graduate degree is a prerequisite for becoming a university professor or researcher. It may also lead to a higher level job within an engineering department or firm. Some companies encourage their employees to pursue graduate education by offering tuition-reimbursement programs. Because technology is rapidly developing, mechanical engineers need to continue their education, formally or informally, throughout their careers. Conferences, seminars, and professional journals serve to educate engineers about developments in the field.

Certification or Licensing

Engineers whose work may affect the life, health, or safety of the public must be registered according to regulations in all 50 states and the District of Columbia. Applicants for registration must have received a degree from an accredited engineering program and have four years of experience. They must also pass a written examination.

Many mechanical engineers also become certified. Certification is a status granted by a technical or professional organization for the purpose of recognizing and documenting an individual's abilities in a specific engineering field. For example, the Society of Manufacturing Engineers offers the following designations to mechanical engineers who work in manufacturing and who meet education and experience requirements: certified manufacturing engineer and certified engineer manager.

Other Requirements

Personal qualities essential for mechanical engineers include the ability to think analytically, to solve problems, and to work with abstract ideas. Attention to detail is also important, as are good oral and written communication skills and the ability to work well in groups. Computer literacy is essential.

EXPLORING

One of the best ways to learn about the field is to talk with a mechanical engineer. It might also be helpful to tour an aerospace manufacturing plant or visit a museum specializing in space science, such as the Smithsonian National Air and Space Museum. Public libraries usually have books on mechanical engineering that might be enlightening. You might tackle a design or building project to test your aptitude for the field. Finally, some high schools offer engineering clubs or organizations. Membership in JETS, the Junior

Engineering Technical Society (http://www.jets.org), is suggested for prospective mechanical engineers.

EMPLOYERS

Approximately 13,300 mechanical engineers are employed in aerospace product and parts manufacturing in the United States. They work for private engineering and aerospace companies and government entities such as NASA and the U.S. Department of Defense. Mechanical engineers also work in a variety of other settings; manufacturers of industrial and office machinery, farm equipment, automobiles, petroleum, pharmaceuticals, fabricated metal products, pulp and paper, electronics, utilities, computers, soap and cosmetics, and heating, ventilating, and air-conditioning systems all employ mechanical engineers. Others are self-employed or work for colleges and universities.

STARTING OUT

Many mechanical engineers find their first job through their college or university career services office. Many companies send recruiters to college campuses to interview and sign up engineering graduates. Other students might find a position in the company where they had a summer or part-time job. Newspapers and professional journals often list job openings for engineers. Job seekers who wish to work for NASA should visit http://www.nasajobs.nasa.gov for more information.

ADVANCEMENT

As engineers gain experience, they can advance to jobs with a wider scope of responsibility and higher pay. Some of these higher-level jobs include technical service and development officers, team leaders, research directors, and managers. Some mechanical engineers use their technical knowledge in sales and marketing positions, while others form their own engineering business or consulting firm.

Many engineers advance by furthering their education. A master's degree in business administration, in addition to an engineering degree, is sometimes helpful in obtaining an administrative position. A master's or doctoral degree in an engineering specialty may also lead to executive work. In addition, those with graduate degrees often have the option of research or teaching positions.

EARNINGS

The National Association of Colleges and Employers reports the following 2005 starting salaries for mechanical engineers by educational achievement: bachelor's degree, $50,236; master's degree, $59,880; and Ph.D., $68,299. The U.S. Department of Labor reports that mechanical engineers employed in aerospace product and parts manufacturing earned mean annual salaries of $62,880 in 2005. Salaries for mechanical engineers employed in all industries ranged from less than $44,550 to $101,660 or more in 2005. Engineers employed by NASA earned starting salaries that ranged from $33,151 to $44,034 in 2006.

Like most professionals, mechanical engineers who work for a company or for a government agency such as NASA usually receive a generous benefits package, including vacation days, sick leave, health and life insurance, and a savings and pension program. Self-employed mechanical engineers must provide their own benefits.

WORK ENVIRONMENT

The working conditions of mechanical engineers vary. Most work indoors in offices, research laboratories, or production departments of factories and shops. Depending on the job, however, a significant amount of work time may be spent on a noisy factory floor, at a construction site, or at another field operation. Mechanical engineers have traditionally designed systems on drafting boards, but since the introduction of sophisticated software programs, design is increasingly done on computers.

Engineering is for the most part a cooperative effort. While the specific duties of an engineer may require independent work, each project is typically the job of an engineering team. Such a team might include other engineers, engineering technicians, and engineering technologists.

Mechanical engineers generally have a 40-hour workweek; however, their working hours are often dictated by project deadlines. They may work long hours to meet a deadline or show up on a second or third shift to check production at a factory or a construction project.

Mechanical engineering can be a very satisfying occupation. Engineers often get the pleasure of seeing their designs or modifications put into actual, tangible form, such as a satellite system or a new type of spacecraft. Conversely, it can be frustrating when a project is stalled, full of errors, or even abandoned completely.

OUTLOOK

The employment of mechanical engineers in aerospace product and parts manufacturing is expected to grow more slowly than the average for all occupations through 2014, according to the U.S. Department of Labor (USDL). Although overall employment in manufacturing is expected to decline, engineers will be needed to meet the demand for more efficient industrial machinery and machine tools. The USDL predicts good opportunities for mechanical engineers who are involved with new technologies such as biotechnology, nanotechnology, and materials science. It should also be noted that increases in defense spending in the wake of the terrorist attacks of September 11, 2001 may create improved employment opportunities for engineers within the federal government.

FOR MORE INFORMATION

For a list of engineering programs at colleges and universities, contact
Accreditation Board for Engineering and Technology
111 Market Place, Suite 1050
Baltimore, MD 21202-7116
Tel: 410-347-7700
http://www.abet.org

Contact the AIA for publications with information on aerospace technologies, careers, and space.
Aerospace Industries Association (AIA)
1000 Wilson Boulevard, Suite 1700
Arlington, VA 22209-3928
Tel: 703-358-1000
http://www.aia-aerospace.org

For career information and information on student branches of this organization, contact the AIAA.
American Institute of Aeronautics and Astronautics (AIAA)
1801 Alexander Bell Drive, Suite 500
Reston, VA 20191-4344
Tel: 800-639-2422
http://www.aiaa.org

For information on mechanical engineering and mechanical engineering technology, contact
American Society of Mechanical Engineers
Three Park Avenue

New York, NY 10016-5990
Tel: 800-843-2763
Email: infocentral@asme.org
http://www.asme.org

For career and scholarship information, contact
General Aviation Manufacturers Association
1400 K Street, NW, Suite 801
Washington, DC 20005-2402
Tel: 202-393-1500
http://www.generalaviation.org

For information about careers and high school engineering competitions, contact
Junior Engineering Technical Society
1420 King Street, Suite 405
Alexandria, VA 22314-2794
Tel: 703-548-5387
Email: info@jets.org
http://www.jets.org

For information on certification, contact
Society of Manufacturing Engineers
One SME Drive
Dearborn, MI 48121-2408
Tel: 800-733-4763
http://www.sme.org

SEDS is an international organization of high school and college students dedicated to promoting interest in space. Its national headquarters are located at the Massachusetts Institute of Technology.
Students for the Exploration and Development of Space (SEDS)
MIT Room W20-401
77 Massachusetts Avenue
Cambridge, MA 02139-4307
Email: mitseds-officers@mit
http://www.mit.edu/~mitseds

Pilots

OVERVIEW

Pilots work in many different kinds of flying jobs. Most people are very familiar with the career of airline pilot, but other pilots are employed in the aerospace and aviation industries. This article focuses on the work of pilots in these industries.

HISTORY

The age of modern aviation is generally considered to have begun with the famous flight of Orville and Wilbur Wright's heavier-than-air machine on December 17, 1903. On that day, the Wright brothers flew their machine four times and became the first airplane pilots.

Aviation developed rapidly as designers raced to improve upon the Wright brothers' design. In addition to commercial developments, airplanes were quickly adapted to military use. As airplanes grew more complex and an entire industry developed, pilots were needed to test and evaluate aircraft.

During World War I, the U.S. Army began testing aircraft via the Aviation Section of the U.S. Army Signal Corps. Realizing that its air force and testing abilities lagged in comparison to those of its European counterparts, the Army established a dedicated aeronautical research and development facility in San Diego, California, in 1914.

In the 1920s, the National Advisory Committee for Aeronautics (which later became the National Aeronautics and Space Administration) also began conducting flight tests.

In the 1940s, the U.S. Air Force and U.S. Navy established flight test training facilities and schools. By the late 1950s, the U.S. Air Force's test pilot school also began to train pilots to become astronauts. The Air Force continued this training until the early 1970s, when NASA took over space-oriented flight test programs and the Air Force test pilot school returned to its original mandate—training military test pilots.

Today, the U.S. Air Force Test Pilot School and the U.S. Naval Test Pilot School continue to train military test pilots.

Working as a test pilot for the military or private companies is not the only job option in the aviation and aerospace industries. Pilots may also work as military pilots, space shuttle pilots, flight instructors, and facilities-flight-check pilots.

THE JOB

Pilots play a key role in the aviation and aerospace industries. The following paragraphs detail available opportunities.

Test pilots play an important role in the testing and development of new aircraft and related technologies. They are employed by aerospace companies, the National Aeronautics and Space Administration (NASA), and the U.S. military, primarily the Air Force and the Navy. Combining knowledge of flying with a background in aeronautical engineering, they test new models of planes and make sure they function properly. When testing an aircraft, test pilots perform precise maneuvers and record how the aircraft responds during every step of the flight—from takeoff to landing. They test dozens of systems, including main and auxiliary power; fire suppression; power drive; propulsion control; communications; computers; fuel delivery; hydraulics/flight controls; environmental control; pneumatic; thermal management; acoustics; and radar. In addition to test-flying aircraft, test pilots participate in flight-simulator testing. They work closely with researchers and spend a considerable amount of time writing detailed reports about the performance of the aircraft and its various systems. The reports are used by aerospace companies and government agencies to determine the feasibility of production, as well as any necessary design modifications. Test pilots are sometimes called *research pilots, research test pilots,* and *experimental test pilots.*

Military pilots fly various types of specialized aircraft to transport troops and equipment and to execute combat missions. Military pilots often go on to become test pilots for the U.S. military, NASA, or private aerospace and aviation companies. Others become astronauts.

Flight instructors are pilots who teach others how to fly. They teach in classrooms or provide in-flight instruction.

Facilities-flight-check pilots fly specially equipped planes to test air navigational aids, air traffic controls, and communications equipment and to evaluate installation sites for such equipment.

Space shuttle pilots are highly trained professionals who pilot the space shuttle on scientific- and defense-related missions. They are members of the U.S. military or employees of NASA.

In addition to actually flying the aircraft, all pilots must perform a variety of safety-related tasks. Before each flight, they must determine weather and flight conditions, ensure that sufficient fuel is on board to complete the flight safely, and verify the maintenance status of the aircraft. Pilots must also perform system-operation checks to test the proper functioning of instrumentation, controls, and electronic and mechanical systems on the flight deck.

Once all preflight duties have been performed, the pilot taxis the aircraft to the designated runway and prepares for takeoff. Takeoff speeds must be calculated based on the aircraft's weight. The aircraft's systems, levers, and switches must be in proper position for takeoff. After takeoff, the pilots may engage an electrical device known as the autopilot. This device can be programmed to maintain the desired course and altitude. With or without the aid of the autopilot, pilots must constantly monitor the aircraft's systems.

Because pilots may encounter turbulence, emergencies, and other hazardous situations during a flight, good judgment and quick response are extremely important. Pilots receive periodic training and evaluation on their handling of in-flight abnormalities and emergencies and on their operation of the aircraft during challenging weather conditions. As a further safety measure, airline pilots are expected to adhere to checklist procedures in all areas of flight operations.

During flights, pilots monitor aircraft systems, keep a watchful eye on local weather conditions, perform checklists, and maintain constant communication with the air traffic controllers along the flight route. The busiest times for pilots are during takeoff and landing. The weather conditions at the aircraft's destination must be obtained and analyzed. The aircraft must be maneuvered and properly configured to make a landing on the runway. When cloud cover is low and visibility is poor, pilots rely solely on the instruments on the flight deck. These instruments include an altimeter and an artificial horizon. Pilots select the appropriate radio navigation frequencies and corresponding course for the ground-based radio

A pilot prepares for flight in the rear station of a T–38 trainer jet. *(NASA)*

and microwave signals that provide horizontal (and in some cases vertical) guidance to the landing runway.

REQUIREMENTS

High School

All prospective pilots must complete high school. A college-preparatory curriculum (science, mathematics, physics, computers, and physical education will be the most helpful) is recommended because of the need for pilots to have at least some college education. Science and mathematics are two important subjects, and you should also take advantage of any computer courses offered. You can start pursuing your pilot's license while in high school.

Postsecondary Training

Flying can be learned in either military or civilian flying schools. There are approximately 600 civilian flying schools certified by the Federal Aviation Administration (FAA), including some colleges and universities that offer degree credit for pilot training. Most state-supported colleges and universities have aviation programs, as do many private schools. Some schools focus solely on aviation education, such as Embry-Riddle Aeronautical University and the University of North Dakota's Center for Aerospace Sciences.

If you are interested in becoming a pilot through military training, you may want to attend one of the four service academies: the U.S. Air Force Academy (for the air force), the U.S. Military Academy (for the army), the U.S. Naval Academy (for the navy and the marines), or the U.S. Coast Guard Academy (for the coast guard). Another option is to attend a four-year postsecondary institution that has a Reserve Officers Training Corps program. Each branch of the Armed Services has specific training requirements for its military pilots. Training in all branches will include flight simulation, classroom training, and basic flight instruction. For more information on specific requirements, contact a recruiter for the branch in which you are interested in entering.

Test pilots receive their training at civilian flight schools, such as the National Test Pilot School, or via military flight test schools (the U.S. Air Force Test Pilot School or the U.S. Naval Test Pilot School). Typical classes include Introduction to Flight Testing; Performance/Flying Qualities and Systems; Avionics Systems; Operational Test and Evaluation; Night Vision Imaging System Evaluation Techniques; Crew Resource Management; and Flight Test Electro-Optic/Infrared Systems.

Certification or Licensing
The military does not offer certification or licensing for military pilots. During the advanced portion of your civilian flight training, though, you must pass the FAA's guidelines and regulations. If you hope to transfer your military skills to a similar job in the civilian sector (for example, with an aviation or aerospace company), you may need additional training and/or certification or licensing.

Other Requirements
Pilots, especially test pilots and space shuttle pilots, must remain calm and level-headed, no matter how trying the situation. They must also have excellent critical thinking and observational skills and be detail oriented. Sound physical and emotional health is an essential requirement for aspiring pilots. Pilots must have 20/20 vision with or without glasses; good hearing; normal heart rate and blood pressure; and no physical handicaps that could hinder performance.

EXPLORING
High school students interested in flying may join a high school aviation club. At 16 years of age, you may start taking flying

Learn More About It

Chaikin, Andrew. *Space: A History Of Space Exploration In Photographs*. Richmond Hill, Ontario: Firefly Books Ltd., 2004.

Dasch, E. Julius, and Ian Ridpath. (eds.) *A Dictionary of Space Exploration*. New York: Oxford University Press, 2006.

Evans, Ben. *Space Shuttle Columbia: Her Missions and Crews*. New York: Springer, 2005.

Furniss, Tim. *A History of Space Exploration*. Guilford, Conn.: Lyons Press, 2006.

Hansen, James R. *First Man: The Life of Neil A. Armstrong*. New York: Simon & Schuster, 2005.

Shayler, David J., and Ian A. Moule. *Women in Space: Following Valentina*. New York: Springer, 2005.

Thomas, Kenneth S., and Harold J. McMann. *US Spacesuits*. New York: Springer, 2005.

lessons. You can also read books and magazines about aviation and visit Web sites that discuss career opportunities for pilots (see "For More Information").

EMPLOYERS

Pilots are employed by the U.S. military, NASA and other government agencies (such as the FAA), and private aviation and aerospace companies. Other pilots are employed by commercial airlines (including both passenger and cargo transport companies) and private companies.

STARTING OUT

Pilots interested in working for private aviation and aerospace companies should contact these companies directly for information on employment opportunities. Job seekers who wish to work for NASA should visit http://www.nasajobs.nasa.gov for more information on available positions.

Once you've decided to become a military pilot, you should contact a military recruiter. The recruiter will help answer questions and suggest different options. To start out in any branch of the military, you must pass medical and physical tests, the Armed Services Vocational Aptitude Battery exam, and basic training. You must also sign an enlistment contract. This is a legal agreement that will bind you to a certain amount of military service, usually eight years. Active duty composes two to six years of this agreement, and the remainder is normally spent in the reserves.

ADVANCEMENT

Test pilots employed by aviation and aerospace companies might advance by being assigned to test more advanced aircraft or by being placed in charge of other pilots. Others may pursue opportunities at larger companies.

Pilots employed by NASA might advance by becoming managers of pilots or by pursuing other career options in the administration.

Military pilots advance by receiving promotions. Each military branch has 10 officers' grades (O-1 through O-10). The higher the number, the more advanced a person's rank. The various branches of the military have somewhat different criteria for promoting individuals; in general, however, promotions depend on factors such as length of time served, demonstrated abilities, recommendations, and scores on written exams. Promotions become more and more competitive as people advance in rank. Military pilots may train for different aircraft and missions. Eventually, they may advance to senior officer or command positions. Military pilots with superior skills and training may advance to the position of astronaut.

Pilots might also choose to leave the aviation and aerospace industries to work as commercial pilots. Pilots employed by commercial airlines may advance to the position of *check pilot,* testing other pilots for advanced ratings; *chief pilot,* supervising the work of other pilots; or to administrative or executive positions with a commercial airline (ground operations). They may also become self-employed, opening a flying business, such as a flight instruction, agricultural aviation, air-taxi, or charter service.

EARNINGS

Pilots (not including astronauts) employed by NASA earned starting salaries that ranged from $31,195 to $74,773 in 2006. Astronauts (including space shuttle pilots) earn salaries in accordance with the U.S. government pay scale. Astronauts enter the field at a minimum classification of GS-11, which in 2006 paid a minimum of $46,189, according to the Office of Personnel Management General Schedule. As they gain experience, astronauts may advance up the classification chart to peak at GS-13, which paid between $65,832 and $85,578 in 2006.

All military pilots serve as officers in their respective branches. According to the Defense Finance and Accounting Service, officers starting out at a grade of O-1 received basic monthly pay of $2,416.20 in 2006. This would make for an annual salary of approximately $28,994.40. An officer with the grade O-5 and more than four years of experience earned $5,177.10 per month or approximately $62,125.20 per year. And an officer with the top grade of O-10 and more than 20 years of experience had monthly basic earnings of $13,365 or approximately $160,380 annually.

In addition to pay, pilots usually receive benefits, including vacations, sick leave, health insurance, retirement pensions, and bonuses for superior performance. Salaries for space shuttle pilots who are members of the armed forces consist of base pay, an allowance for housing and subsistence, and flight pay. Additional benefits for military workers include uniform allowances, 30 days' paid vacation time per year, and the opportunity to retire after 20 years of service. Generally, those retiring will receive 40 percent of the average of the highest three years of their base pay. This amount rises incrementally, reaching 75 percent of the average of the highest three years of base pay after 30 years of service. All retirement provisions are subject to change, however, and you should verify them as well as current salary information before you enlist. Military pilots who retire after 20 years of service are usually in their 40s and thus have plenty of time, as well as an accumulation of skills, with which to start a second career as a civilian pilot or in a related field.

WORK ENVIRONMENT

While being a pilot can be a rewarding career, it can also be extremely stressful. During flights, they must concentrate on a variety of factors. They must always be alert to changes in conditions and to any problems that may occur. Test pilots have the additional responsibility of assessing the performance of their aircraft and its systems during takeoff, flight, and landing. During emergencies, pilots must react quickly, logically, and decisively. Pilots often work irregular hours, may be away from home a lot, and are subject to jet lag and other conditions associated with flying.

The work environment for military pilots is rewarding, varied, and sometimes stressful. Pilots may be assigned to one or more air bases around the world. They may take off and land on aircraft carriers, at conventional airports, in desert conditions under fierce fire from the enemy, or in countless other settings. They may fly the same routes for extended periods of time, but no two flights are ever the same.

OUTLOOK

Aviation and aerospace technology is constantly evolving, and test pilots will be needed to test cutting-edge aircraft. Although unmanned aerial vehicles have reduced the need for some test pilots, industry experts predict that test pilots will continue to play a very important role in the testing and analysis of aircraft.

Although budgets at NASA have declined in recent years, there is no doubt that pilots will still be needed. Pilots are an integral part of the space program. NASA plans to retire the space shuttle by 2010, but pilots will be needed to fly its replacement, the Crew Exploration Vehicle.

The outlook for military workers, including military pilots, is expected to be good through 2014, according to the U.S. Department of Labor. While political and economic conditions will have an influence on the military's duties and employment outlook, the country will always need military pilots, both for defense and to protect its interests and citizens around the world.

FOR MORE INFORMATION

Contact the AIA for publications with information on aerospace technologies, careers, and space.
Aerospace Industries Association (AIA)
1000 Wilson Boulevard, Suite 1700
Arlington, VA 22209-3928
Tel: 703-358-1000
http://www.aia-aerospace.org

For career information and information on student branches of this organization, contact the AIAA.
American Institute of Aeronautics and Astronautics (AIAA)
1801 Alexander Bell Drive, Suite 500
Reston, VA 20191-4344
Tel: 800-639-2422
http://www.aiaa.org

For information on experimental aircraft, contact
Experimental Aircraft Association (EAA)
EAA Aviation Center

3000 Poberezny Road
Oshkosh, WI 54902-8939
Tel: 920-426-4800
http://www.eaa.org

For information on aeronautical careers, internships, and student projects, contact the information center or visit NASA's Web site.
National Aeronautics and Space Administration (NASA)
Public Communications and Inquiries Management Office,
  Suite 1M32
Washington, DC 20546-0001
Tel: 202-358-0001
Email: public-inquiries@hq.nasa.gov
http://www.nasa.gov

For information on scholarships, contact
Society of Experimental Test Pilots
PO Box 986
Lancaster, CA 93584-0986
Tel: 661-942-9574
Email: Setp@setp.org
http://www.setp.org

For more information on flight testing, visit the following Web site:
**NASA Dryden Flight Research Center's Introduction to Flight
  Test Maneuvers**
http://www.dfrc.nasa.gov/Education/OnlineEd/Intro2Flight

Visit the following Web sites for information on test pilot schools:
National Test Pilot School
http://www.ntps.com

U.S. Air Force Test Pilot School
http://www.edwards.af.mil/tps

U.S. Naval Test Pilot School
http://www.usntps.navy.mil

For a wealth of information on flight testing, visit the following Web site:
Test Pilot Stuff
http://www.testpilots.com

Robotics Engineers and Technicians

OVERVIEW

Robotics engineers design, develop, build, and program robots and robotic devices, including peripheral equipment and computer software used to control robots. *Robotics technicians* assist robotics engineers in a wide variety of tasks relating to the design, development, production, testing, operation, repair, and maintenance of robots and robotic devices. Robots are used widely in the aerospace industry for space exploration and to assist in the manufacturing of aircraft and spacecraft.

HISTORY

Robots are devices that perform tasks ordinarily performed by humans; they seem to operate with an almost-human intelligence. The idea of robots can be traced back to the ancient Greek and Egyptian civilizations. An inventor from the first century AD, Hero of Alexandria, invented a machine that would automatically open the doors of a temple when the priest lit a fire in the altar. During the later periods of the Middle Ages, the Renaissance, and the 17th and 18th centuries, interest in robot-like mechanisms turned mostly to automatons, devices that imitate human and animal appearance and activity but perform no useful task.

The Industrial Revolution inspired the invention of many different kinds of automatic machinery. One of the most important robotics inventions occurred in 1804: Joseph-Marie Jacquard's method for controlling machinery by means of a programmed set of instructions recorded on a punched paper tape that was fed into a machine to direct its movements.

The word *robot* and the concepts associated with it were first introduced in the early 1920s. They made their appearance in a play titled *R.U.R.*, which stands for Rossum's Universal Robots, written by Czechoslovakian dramatist Karel Capek. The play involves human-like robotic machines created to perform manual tasks for their human masters.

During the 1950s and 1960s, advances in the fields of automation and computer science led to the development of experimental robots that could imitate a wide range of human activity, including self-regulated and self-propelled movement (either on wheels or on legs), the ability to sense and manipulate objects, and the ability to select a course of action on the basis of conditions around them.

In 1954, George Devol designed the first programmable robot in the United States. He named it the Universal Automation, which was later shortened to Unimation, which also became the name of the first robot company. Hydraulic robots, controlled by numerical control programming, were developed in the 1960s and were used initially by the automobile industry in assembly line operations. By 1973, robots were being built with electric power and electronic controls, which allowed greater flexibility and increased uses.

Robotic technology has evolved significantly in the past few decades. Early robotic equipment, often referred to as first-generation robots, consisted of simple mechanical arms or devices that could perform precise, repetitive motions at high speeds. It contained no artificial intelligence capabilities. Second-generation robots, which came into use in the 1980s, are controlled by minicomputers and programmed by computer language. They contain sensors, such as vision systems and pressure, proximity, and tactile sensors, which provide information about the outside environment. Third-generation robots, also controlled by minicomputers and equipped with sensory devices, are currently being developed. Referred to as "smart" robots, they can work on their own without supervision by an external computer or human being.

The evolution of robots is closely tied to the study of human anatomy and movement of the human body. The early robots were modeled after arms, then wrists. Second-generation robots include features that model human hands. Third-generation robots are being developed with legs and complex joint technology. They also incorporate multisensory input controls, such as ultrasonic sensors or sensors that can "sniff" and "taste."

THE JOB

The majority of robotics engineers and technicians work within the field of computer-integrated manufacturing or programmable automation. Using computer science technology, engineers design and develop robots and other automated equipment, including computer software used to program robots.

The title "robotics engineer" may be used to refer to any engineer who works primarily with robots. Oftentimes, their educational background lies within the many engineering specialties—mechanical, electrical, computer, or manufacturing. There has been, in recent times, a growing number of engineering professionals graduating with a degree in robotics engineering.

Robotics engineers have a thorough understanding of robotic systems and equipment and know the different technologies available to create robots for specific applications. They must be knowledgeable of computers and computer systems and how they can be used to control and navigate robotic equipment. Robotics engineers must also be aware of manufacturing production requirements to ensure cost effectiveness and efficiency. Many times, engineers need to provide evidence that robots are better suited for a job over human beings in terms of safety, performance, or cost. To provide just one example, engineers employed by the National Aeronautics and Space Administration (NASA) may be assigned to the Mars Exploration Program to develop, maintain, and operate the Mars Exploration Rovers (MERs). These small robots have explored the planet, gathered samples, and captured images used for research on Earth. MERs are often used in planetary exploration as they are less expensive and safer than sending human explorers. Robotic engineers are involved in the design, manufacturing, and operation of the mechanical systems of the MERs in order to achieve maximum mobility, accuracy, and efficiency. They also research, design, and develop the electrical systems used in these robots and their power supply. They may specialize in areas such as integrated circuit theory, lasers, electronic sensors, optical components, and energy power systems. They are also responsible for the design of the computer systems used to program the MERs. Computer systems enable workers at NASA headquarters to maneuver the MERs during collection of soil or rock samples, or to navigate the MERs to a different location on the planet.

In addition to their work on exploration rovers, robotics engineers might focus on robotic systems on the space shuttle, the International Space System, satellites, and those required in defense-related technology.

Many times, robotics engineers are assisted by robotics technicians in all phases of a project—design, installation, and repair.

REQUIREMENTS

High School
In high school, you should take as many science, math, and computer classes as possible. Recommended courses include biology, chemistry, physics, algebra, trigonometry, geometry, calculus, graphics, computer science, English, speech, composition, social studies, and drafting. In addition, take shop and vocational classes that teach blueprint and electrical schematic reading, the use of hand tools, drafting, and the basics of electricity and electronics.

Postsecondary Training
Because changes occur so rapidly within this field, it is recommended that engineers and technicians get a broad-based education that encompasses robotics but does not focus solely on robotics. Programs that provide the widest career base are those in automated manufacturing, which includes robotics, electronics, and computer science.

In order to become an engineer, it is necessary to earn a bachelor of science degree, which generally takes four or five years to complete. More than 400 colleges and universities offer courses in robotics or related technology. Many different types of programs are available. Some colleges and universities offer robotics engineering degrees and others offer engineering degrees with concentrations or options in robotics and manufacturing engineering. For some higher-level jobs, such as robotics designer, a master of science or doctoral degree is required. Carnegie Mellon University has an extensive robotics program and offers an undergraduate minor, as well as master's and doctoral degrees in robotics. Visit http://robotics.nasa.gov/students/robo_u.php for a list of colleges and universities that offer educational programs in robotics.

Although the minimum educational requirement for a robotics technician is a high school diploma, many employers prefer to hire technicians who have received formal training beyond high school. Two-year programs are available in community colleges and technical institutes that grant an associate's degree in robotics. The armed forces also offer technical programs that result in associate's degrees in electronics, biomedical equipment, and computer science. The military uses robotics and other advanced equipment and offers excellent training opportunities to members of the armed forces. This training is highly regarded by many employers and can be an advantage in obtaining a civilian job in robotics.

Other Requirements

Because the field of robotics is rapidly changing, one of the most important requirements for a person interested in a career in robotics is the willingness to pursue additional training on an ongoing basis during his or her career. After completing their formal education, engineers and technicians may need to take additional classes in a college or university or take advantage of training offered through their employers and professional associations.

Robotics engineers and technicians need manual dexterity, good hand-eye coordination, and mechanical and electrical aptitude.

EXPLORING

Because robotics is a relatively new field, it is important to learn as much as possible about current trends and recent technologies. Reading books and articles in trade magazines provides an excellent way to learn about what is happening in robotics technologies and expected future trends. Trade magazines with informative articles include *Robotics Engineering; Robotics and Autonomous Systems; and Unmanned Systems.*

You can become a robot hobbyist and build your own robots or buy toy robots and experiment with them. Complete robot kits are available through a number of companies and range from simple, inexpensive robots to highly complex robots with advanced features and accessories. A number of books that give instructions and helpful hints on building robots can be found at most public libraries and bookstores. In addition, relatively inexpensive and simple toy robots are available from electronics shops, department stores, and mail order companies.

You can also participate in competitions. The International Aerial Robotics Competition is sponsored by the Association for Unmanned Vehicle Systems International. This competition, which requires teams of students to build complex robots, is open to college students. (Visit http://avdil.gtri.gatech.edu/AUVS/IARCLaunchPoint. html for more information)

Participating in summer camps is another great way to explore the field. Visit http://robotics.nasa.gov/students/camp.php to learn more about camps offered by NASA and other organizations.

Another great way to learn about robotics is to attend trade shows. Many robotics and automated machinery manufacturers

Learn More About It

Cook, David. *Robot Building for Beginners.* Berkeley, Calif.: Apress, 2002.

Craig, John J. *Introduction to Robotics: Mechanics and Control.* 3rd ed. Upper Saddle River, N.J.: Prentice Hall, 2003.

Ellery, Alex. *An Introduction to Space Robotics.* New York: Springer, 2000.

Hrynkiw, Dave and Mark W. Tilden. *JunkBots, Bugbots, and Bots on Wheels: Building Simple Robots with BEAM Technology.* Emeryville, Calif.: McGraw-Hill/Osborne Media, 2002.

Lunt, Karl. *Build Your Own Robot!* Natick, Mass.: A K Peters Ltd., 2000.

Martin, Fred. *Robotic Explorations: An Introduction to Engineering Through Design.* Upper Saddle River, N.J.: Prentice Hall, 2000.

McComb, Gordon, and Myke Predko. *Robot Builder's Bonanza.* 3rd ed. New York: McGraw-Hill/TAB Electronics, 2006.

McComb, Gordon. *Robot Builder's Sourcebook: Over 2,500 Sources for Robot Parts.* New York: McGraw-Hill/TAB Electronics, 2002.

Ulivi, Paolo, and David M. Harland. *Lunar Exploration: Human Pioneers and Robotic Surveyors.* New York: Springer, 2004.

exhibit their products at shows and conventions. Numerous such trade shows are held every year in different parts of the country. Information about these trade shows is available through association trade magazines and periodicals such as *Managing Automation* (http://www.managingautomation.com).

Other activities that foster knowledge and skills relevant to a career in robotics include membership in high school science clubs, participation in science fairs, and pursuing hobbies that involve electronics, mechanical equipment, and model building.

EMPLOYERS

Robotics engineers and technicians are employed in virtually every manufacturing industry, including those that produce products for the aviation and aerospace industries. A large number of robotics manufacturers are found in California, Michigan, Illinois, Indiana,

Pennsylvania, Ohio, Connecticut, Texas, British Columbia, and Ontario, although companies exist in many other states and parts of Canada. NASA and other government agencies also employ a significant number of robotics engineers and technicians. With the trend toward automation continuing—often via the use of robots—people trained in robotics can expect to find employment with almost all types of manufacturing companies, as well as many government agencies, in the future.

STARTING OUT

In the past, most people entered robotics technician positions from positions as automotive workers, machinists, millwrights, computer repair technicians, and computer operators. Companies retrained them to troubleshoot and repair robots rather than hire new workers. Although this still occurs today, there are many more opportunities for formal education and training specifically in robotics engineering, and robotics manufacturers are more likely to hire graduates of robotics programs, both at the technician and engineer levels.

Graduates of two- and four-year programs may learn about available openings through their schools' job placement services. It also may be possible to learn about job openings through want ads in newspapers and trade magazines.

In many cases, it will be necessary to research companies that manufacture or use robots and apply directly to them. The organizations listed at the end of this article may offer publications with classified ads or other job search information.

Job opportunities may be good at small start-up companies or a start-up robotics unit of a large company. Many times, these employers are willing to hire inexperienced workers as apprentices or assistants. Then, when their sales and production grow, these workers have the best chances for advancement.

Job seekers who wish to work for NASA should visit http://www.nasajobs.nasa.gov for more information.

Other places to search for employment include your college's job placement services, advertisements in professional magazines and newspapers, or job fairs.

ADVANCEMENT

Engineers may start as part of an engineering team and do relatively simple tasks under the supervision of a project manager or more experienced engineer. With experience and demonstrated competency, they can move into higher engineering positions. Engineers who demonstrate good interpersonal skills, leadership abilities, and technical expertise may become team leaders, project managers, or chief engineers. Engineers can also move into supervisory or management positions. Some engineers pursue an MBA (master of business administration) degree. These engineers are able to move into top management positions. Some engineers also develop specialties such as artificial intelligence and move into highly specialized engineering positions.

After several years on the job, robotics technicians who have demonstrated their ability to handle more responsibility may be assigned some supervisory work or, more likely, will train new technicians. Experienced technicians and engineers may teach courses at their workplace or find teaching opportunities at a local school or community college.

Other routes for advancement include becoming a sales representative for a robotics manufacturing or design firm or working as an independent contractor for companies that use or manufacture robots.

With additional training and education, such as a bachelor's degree, technicians can become eligible for positions as robotics engineers.

EARNINGS

Earnings and benefits vary widely based on the size of the company, geographic location, nature of the production process, and complexity of the robots. In general, engineers with a bachelor of science degree earn annual salaries between $49,000 and $52,000 in their first job after graduation. According to the U.S. Department of Labor, mechanical engineers employed in aerospace product and parts manufacturing earned mean annual salaries of $62,880 in 2005. Median annual earnings of computer hardware engineers were $84,420, and mean annual earnings of electronics engineers, except computer engineers, who were employed in aerospace product and parts manufacturing were $89,880. All of these engineers can earn annual salaries well over $100,000 with increased experience and responsibility.

Robotics technicians who are graduates of a two-year robotics program earn between $26,000 and $35,000 a year. With increased training and experience, technicians can earn $50,000 or more. The U.S. Department of Labor reports that mean annual earnings of electrical and electronics engineering technicians who were employed in aerospace product and parts manufacturing were $58,400 in 2005. The average annual salary for mechanical engineering technicians employed in all industries was $44,830 in 2005. Technicians with considerable experience and a college degree can earn $65,000 or more.

Employers offer a variety of benefits that can include the following: paid holidays, vacations, personal days, and sick leave; medical, dental, disability, and life insurance; 401 (k) plans, pension and retirement plans; profit sharing; and educational assistance programs.

WORK ENVIRONMENT

Robotics engineers and technicians may work either for a company that manufactures robots or a company or government organization (such as NASA) that uses robots. Most companies that manufacture robots are relatively clean, quiet, and comfortable environments. Engineers and technicians may work in an office or on the production floor.

Engineers and technicians who work in a company that uses robots may work in noisy, hot, and dirty surroundings. Others, such as those employed by NASA, may work in clean, well-lighted offices or control rooms. Conditions vary based on the type of industry within which one works. Some robotics personnel are required to work in clean room environments, which keep electronic components free of dirt and other contaminants. Workers in these environments wear face masks, hair coverings, and special protective clothing.

Some engineers and technicians may confront potentially hazardous conditions in the workplace. Robots, after all, are often designed and used precisely because the task they perform involves some risk to humans: handling laser beams, arc-welding equipment, radioactive substances, or hazardous chemicals. When they design, test, build, install, and repair robots, it is inevitable that some engineers and technicians will be exposed to these same risks. Plant safety procedures protect the attentive and cautious worker, but carelessness in such settings can be especially dangerous.

In general, most technicians and engineers work 40-hour workweeks, although overtime may be required for special projects or to repair equipment that is shutting down a production line. Some technicians, particularly those involved in maintenance and repairs, may work shifts that include evening, late night, or weekend work.

Field service technicians travel to manufacturing sites to repair robots. Their work may involve extensive travel and overnight stays. They may work at several sites in one day or stay at one location for an extended period for more difficult repairs.

OUTLOOK

Employment opportunities for robotics engineers and technicians are closely tied to economic conditions in the United States and in the global marketplace. The U.S. Department of Labor predicts the fields of mechanical, electronics, and computer hardware engineering will grow about as fast as the average through 2014, mainly due to increased foreign competition. Job opportunities for engineering technicians will also grow at an average rate. Technicians will be needed to perform many of the essential tasks in existing engineering firms. Competition for both engineering and technician jobs will be stiff, and opportunities will be best for those that have advanced degrees.

FOR MORE INFORMATION

Contact the AIA for publications with information on aerospace technologies, careers, and space.

Aerospace Industries Association (AIA)
1000 Wilson Boulevard, Suite 1700
Arlington, VA 22209-3928
Tel: 703-358-1000
http://www.aia-aerospace.org

For career information and information on student branches of this organization, contact the AIAA.

American Institute of Aeronautics and Astronautics (AIAA)
1801 Alexander Bell Drive, Suite 500
Reston, VA 20191-4344
Tel: 800-639-2422
http://www.aiaa.org

For information on competitions and student membership, contact

Association for Unmanned Vehicle Systems International
2700 South Quincy Street, Suite 400
Arlington, VA 22206-2226
Tel: 703-845-9671
Email: info@auvsi.org
http://www.auvsi.org

For career information, company profiles, training seminars, and educational resources, contact

Robotic Industries Association

900 Victors Way
PO Box 3724
Ann Arbor, MI 48106-2735
Tel: 734-994-6088
http://www.roboticsonline.com

For information on careers and educational programs, contact
Robotics and Automation Society
Institute of Electrical and Electronics Engineers
445 Hoes Lane
Piscataway, NJ 08855-4141
http://www.ncsu.edu/ieee-ras

For information on educational programs, competitions, and student membership in the SME, contact
Society of Manufacturing Engineers (SME)
One SME Drive
Dearborn, MI 48121-2408
Tel: 800-733-4763
http://www.sme.org

SEDS is an international organization of high school and college students dedicated to promoting interest in space. Its national headquarters are located at the Massachusetts Institute of Technology.
Students for the Exploration and Development of Space (SEDS)
MIT Room W20-401
77 Massachusetts Avenue
Cambridge, MA 02139-4307
Email: mitseds-officers@mit
http://www.mit.edu/~mitseds

Visit the following Web site for information on robotics education and summer camps and programs:
The Robotics Alliance Project
National Aeronautics and Space Administration
http://robotics.nasa.gov

Writers, Aerospace/ Aviation

OVERVIEW

Aerospace/aviation writers combine their talent for communication, along with their technical knowledge in engineering, mathematics, aviation, and aerospace science to produce reports, documents, or manuals; write articles for publication in magazines, newspapers, and journals; conduct research; or help market a new product. They are employed by either private companies or government-funded agencies or programs. There are approximately 142,000 salaried writers and authors employed in the United States. Only a small percentage of these writers are employed in the aerospace and aviation industries.

HISTORY

Modern aviation is generally considered to have started with the famous flight of Orville and Wilbur Wright's heavier-than-air machine on December 17, 1903. And with the advent of modern aviation came the need for journalists and writers to educate the public about the exploits of the Wrights and other aviation pioneers, the technology and science behind flight, and ongoing developments in the field. Technical writers with experience in aviation science were also needed to convey the latest findings to industry professionals via trade publications.

The beginnings of astronautics, the science of space flight, followed closely on the heels of the airplane in the early part of the 20th century. The Soviets launched the first successful spacecraft, *Sputnik,* in

1957, and the space age began. From these early forays into space to the multibillion-dollar industry of today, aerospace/aviation writers have played a key role in educating the public and industry professionals about the major developments and breakthroughs in the field.

In 1995, the Royal Aeronautical Society and l'Aero-Club de France created the Aerospace Journalist of the Year Award to recognize top journalists and promote aerospace journalism throughout the world.

In addition to the print media, the broadcasting industry has contributed to the development of the professional aerospace/aviation writer. Radio, television, and the Internet are sources of information, education, and entertainment that provide employment for many writers, including those specializing in aerospace and aviation news.

THE JOB

The aerospace industry encompasses many distinct areas, including unmanned and manned space travel; the manufacturing of aircraft, spacecraft, guided missiles, engines, propulsion units, satellites, exploration vehicles, and other types of equipment and technology; and scientific research in dozens of academic disciplines, including astrobiology, astrogeology, astronomy, astrophysics, chemistry, and engineering. As a result, qualified writers can find a variety of employment possibilities within this exciting field.

Many are employed as technical writers. *Aerospace/aviation technical writers* analyze scientific data in order to generate reports and documents for a particular department or audience. For example, technical writers employed at a company that manufactures business jets could be responsible for writing marketing packets to introduce a new fleet of planes to potential customers. A jet's complicated blueprints and engineering orders would need to be "simplified" or interpreted in a way that would be easily understood by corporate executives interested in purchasing the plane. Technical writers in this position work closely with mathematicians, engineers, and other professionals, acting as a liaison between the marketing department and the scientific community. Others might work in public relations, writing press releases or ghostwriting speeches for company executives.

Technical writers and *aerospace/aviation reporters* are also hired to staff trade journals, such as *Aviation Week & Space Technology* or *Aerospace America,* which cater to the interest of the aerospace and aviation industries. In this capacity, the writers report on developments and advancements such as a new jet-propulsion system that emits less noise pollution, recent increased funding of longer-range self-guided missiles, the future of supersonic business jets, changes in NASA's management structure after the Space Shuttle *Columbia* tragedy, or the emergence of a start-up company taking the aerospace industry by storm. Technical writers work for private companies—such as Boeing, Lockheed Martin, or United Airlines—as well as government-funded agencies such as the National Aeronautics and Space Administration. Other aviation reporters work for popular publications such as *Discover* and *Popular Science*, detailing the latest breakthroughs to the general public.

Some writers can find employment as researchers or analysts for engineering companies that provide products used by the aerospace industry. *Analysts/writers* working at such a company would test, compile results, and create programs for such products as an aviation simulation system to train pilots to handle challenging in-flight situations. Analysts/writers would also work alongside computer scientists and engineers to create manuals and promotional materials for such systems.

REQUIREMENTS
High School
While in high school, build a broad educational foundation by taking courses in English, mathematics, physics, foreign languages, history, general science, social studies, computer science, and typing. The ability to type is almost a requisite for all positions in the communications field, as is familiarity with computers. Take as many writing courses as you can. Strong technical writing skills are essential, of course, for a career as an aerospace/aviation writer.

Postsecondary Training
Competition for writing jobs almost always demands the background of a college education. Many writers prepare for this challenging career by earning at least a bachelor's degree in English; many have degrees in aerospace science, an engineering discipline, mathematics, or a related subject.

In addition to formal course work, most employers look for practical writing experience. If you have served on high school or college newspapers, yearbooks, or literary magazines, you will make a better candidate, as well as if you have worked for small community newspapers or radio stations, even in an unpaid position. Many book publishers, magazines, and newspapers have summer internship programs that provide valuable training if you want to learn about the publishing industry. Interns do many simple tasks, such as running errands and answering phones, but some may be asked to perform research, conduct interviews, or even write some minor pieces.

Other Requirements

To be a writer, you should be creative and able to express ideas clearly, have a broad general knowledge, be skilled in research techniques, and be computer literate. You should also have a strong knowledge of the aerospace, aviation, and related industries. Other assets include curiosity, persistence, initiative, resourcefulness, and an accurate memory. For some jobs—on a newspaper, for example, where the activity is hectic and deadlines are short—the ability to concentrate and produce under pressure is essential.

EXPLORING

As a high school or college student, you can test your interest and aptitude in the field of writing by serving as a reporter or writer on school newspapers, yearbooks, and literary magazines. Various writing courses and workshops will offer you the opportunity to sharpen your writing skills. You should also read popular aerospace/aviation publications to learn about issues in the field (see the sidebar on page 177 for a list of publications).

Small community newspapers and local magazines or trade publications often welcome contributions from outside sources, although they may not have the resources to pay for them. Jobs in bookstores, magazine shops, and even newsstands will offer you a chance to become familiar with various publications.

You can also obtain information on writing as a career by visiting local newspapers, industry trade magazines, publishers, and aerospace companies and interviewing some of the writers who work there. Career conferences and other guidance programs frequently include speakers on the entire field of communications from local or national organizations.

EMPLOYERS

There are approximately 142,000 writers and authors employed in the United States. Only a small percentage of this group works in the aerospace and aviation industries. Nearly 50 percent of salaried writers and editors work for newspaper, periodical,

Aerospace Journals and Magazines

Aerospace America
http://www.aiaa.org/content.cfm?pageid=168

Aerospace Engineering Online
http://sae.org/aeromag

Air & Space
http://airspacemag.com

Aviation Week & Space Technology
http://www.aviationnow.com

Discover
http://www.discover.com

Journal of Guidance, Control, and Dynamics
http://www.aiaa.org/content.cfm?pageid=167

Journal of Propulsion and Power
http://www.aiaa.org/content.cfm?pageid=167

Journal of Spacecraft and Rockets
http://www.aiaa.org/content.cfm?pageid=167

Military Aerospace Technology
http://www.military-aerospace-technology.com

Military & Aerospace Electronics
http://mae.pennnet.com

NASA Technology Briefs
http://www.nasatech.com

Popular Science
http://www.popsci.com/popsci

Space News
http://www.space.com/spacenews

book, and directory publishers; radio and television broadcasting; software publishers; motion picture and sound-recording industries; Internet service providers, Web search portals, and data-processing services; and Internet publishing and broadcasting, according to the *Occupational Outlook Handbook*. Writers are also employed by advertising agencies and public relations firms and for journals and newsletters published by business and nonprofit organizations, such as professional associations, labor unions, and religious organizations. Other employers are government agencies such as NASA.

STARTING OUT

A fair amount of experience is required to gain a high-level position in the field. Most aerospace/aviation writers start out in entry-level positions. These jobs may be listed with college career services offices, or they may be obtained by applying directly to the employment departments of the individual publishers or aerospace/aviation companies. Graduates who previously served internships with these companies often have the advantage of knowing someone who can give them a personal recommendation. Want ads in newspapers and trade journals are another source for jobs. Because of the competition for positions, however, few vacancies are listed with public or private employment agencies.

Employers in the communications field usually are interested in samples of published writing. These are often assembled in an organized portfolio or scrapbook. Bylined or signed articles are more credible (and, as a result, more useful) than stories whose source is not identified.

Beginning positions as a junior writer usually involve library research, preparation of rough drafts for part or all of a report, cataloging, and other related writing tasks. These are generally carried out under the supervision of a senior writer.

ADVANCEMENT

Most aerospace/aviation writers find their first jobs as editorial or production assistants. Advancement may be more rapid in small companies, where beginners learn by doing a little bit of everything and may be given writing tasks immediately. In large firms, duties are usually more compartmentalized. Assistants in entry-level positions are assigned such tasks as research, fact checking, and copyrighting, but it generally takes much longer to advance to full-scale writing duties.

Promotion into more responsible positions may come with the assignment of more important articles and stories to write or may be the result of moving to another company. Mobility among employees in this field is common. An assistant in one publishing house may switch to an executive position in another. Another writer may move from working for a small regional aerospace company to an international company such as Boeing. Or a writer may switch to a related field as a type of advancement.

Freelance or self-employed writers earn advancement in the form of larger fees as they gain exposure and establish their reputations.

Some aerospace journalists are nominated for the Aerospace Journalist of the Year Award. Winners of this prestigious award will find increased employment opportunities, as well as the opportunity to demand higher pay for their work.

EARNINGS

The U.S. Department of Labor does not provide salary information for aerospace/aviation writers, but it does report that the median salary for all technical writers was $55,160 in 2005. The lowest 10 percent earned less than $33,250, while the highest 10 percent earned $87,550 or more. Salaries for writers and authors ranged from less than $24,320 to $89,940 or more.

In addition to their salaries, many aerospace/aviation writers earn some income from freelance work. Part-time freelancers may earn from $5,000 to $15,000 a year. Freelance earnings vary widely. Full-time established freelance writers may earn up to $75,000 a year.

WORK ENVIRONMENT

Working conditions vary for aerospace/aviation writers. Although their workweek usually runs 35 to 40 hours, many writers work overtime. A publication issued frequently has more deadlines closer together, creating greater pressures to meet them. The work is especially hectic on newspapers, which operate seven days a week. Writers often work nights and weekends to meet deadlines or to cover a late-developing story.

Most writers work independently, but they often must cooperate with graphic designers, photographers, rewriters, and advertising people who may have widely differing ideas of how materials should be prepared and presented.

Physical surroundings range from comfortable private offices to noisy, crowded newsrooms filled with other workers typing and talking on the telephone. Some writers must confine their research to the library or telephone interviews, but others may travel to other cities or countries or to local sites such as airports, aerospace companies, and NASA facilities.

The work is arduous, but most aerospace/aviation writers are seldom bored. The most difficult element is the continual pressure of deadlines. People who are the most content as writers enjoy and work well with deadline pressure.

Space Shuttle *Discovery* launches on a two–day mission to the International Space Station, making for a newsworthy story. *(Nathaniel Moore/ U.S. Navy, U.S. Dept. of Defense)*

OUTLOOK

The employment of all writers is expected to increase about as fast as the average rate of all occupations through 2014, according to the U.S. Department of Labor. The demand for writers by newspapers, periodicals, book publishers, and trade associations is expected to increase. The public continues to be fascinated by developments in the aerospace and aviation industries, and talented writers with a strong background in the field will be in demand. The growth of online publishing on company Web sites and other online services will also require many talented writers; those with computer skills will be at an advantage as a result.

FOR MORE INFORMATION

This organization offers student memberships for those interested in opinion writing.

National Conference of Editorial Writers
3899 North Front Street
Harrisburg, PA 17110-1583
Tel: 717-703-3015
Email: ncew@pa-news.org
http://www.ncew.org

For information about working as a writer and union membership, contact
National Writers Union
113 University Place, 6th Floor
New York, NY 10003-4527
Tel: 212-254-0279
Email: nwu@nwu.org
http://www.nwu.org

For information on scholarships and student memberships aimed at those preparing for a career in technical communication, contact
Society for Technical Communication
901 North Stuart Street, Suite 904
Arlington, VA 22203-1821
Tel: 703-522-4114
Email: stc@stc.org
http://www.stc.org

This organization for journalists has campus and online chapters.
Society of Professional Journalists
Eugene S. Pulliam National Journalism Center
3909 North Meridian Street
Indianapolis, IN 46208
Tel: 317-927-8000
http://www.spj.org

Index

Page numbers in bold indicate major treatment of a topic.